GCSE German by RSL

Volume 1: Listening, Speaking

Visit **www.rsleducational.co.uk/germanaudio** to download:

> ➤ Audio material for use with the listening papers in this pack.

> ➤ Example oral exam conversations.

This pack contains:

> ➤ **Four listening papers with detailed solutions**.

> ➤ An **oral (speaking) primer** with advice, marking guidance and analysis of the downloadable sample conversations.

> ➤ *Steps To A Higher Grade*: How to boost your written and oral responses.

The listening papers are modelled on papers set by all exam boards for their 9-1 GCSE/IGCSE syllabuses, and cover an extensive range of topics. The questions become progressively more challenging in each paper, from 'warm-up' questions to more advanced comprehension exercises.

The papers are accompanied by highly detailed, *teaching* solution pages and mark schemes. These will guide you through the questions, step-by-step – like having a personal tutor alongside you.

When used together with *Volume 2: Reading, Writing, Translation*, this pack offers thorough preparation for an excellent performance at GCSE.

How to use this pack

When correcting your work, it's a good idea to take notes of any important learning points, as well as your mistakes: this will make revision easier. If an answer can be improved, it's worthwhile to repeat it, referring to the examples. Where alternative methods and solutions are suggested, it's often useful to try them out – to find out whether they work for you.

You can attempt these papers with or without time limits. Either way, I recommend working though the solution pages carefully, until you fully understand all the advice.

A note on exam boards

These papers are relevant to all exam boards. AQA GCSE and Edexcel (GCSE and IGCSE) exams require some answers to be written in German and some in English, while Cambridge IGCSE focuses on German answers. Therefore, some of the questions in each listening paper ask you to answer in German, and others in English.

I hope you enjoy working through this pack.

We are a family business in a competitive marketplace. We are constantly improving and expanding our range, in order to publish ever-better resources for our customers – in particular, families who find that our books offer better value than expensive private tuition.

If you have any feedback or questions, please let us know! You can get in touch through our website at **www.rsleducational.co.uk**, where you can also view our up-to-date range of publications, or by emailing **robert@rsleducational.co.uk**.

If you like this product, please tell your friends and write a review on Amazon!

Also available

- ➢ GCSE German by RSL, Volume 2: Reading, Writing, Translation
- ➢ GCSE Maths by RSL (Non-Calculator: Higher Level)
- ➢ GCSE Spanish by RSL: Volumes 1 and 2
- ➢ GCSE French by RSL: Volumes 1 and 2
- ➢ RSL 11+ Comprehension: Volumes 1 and 2
- ➢ RSL 11+ Maths
- ➢ RSL 8+ Comprehension
- ➢ RSL 13+ Comprehension
- ➢ *11 Plus Lifeline* (printable comprehension, maths, reasoning and creative writing material): **www.11pluslifeline.com**

GCSE German by RSL, Volume 1: Listening, Speaking
By Matt Lim
Published by RSL Educational
Copyright © RSL Educational Ltd 2019

Table of Contents

Listening Paper 1   5

    Solutions   16

Listening Paper 2   32

    Solutions   44

Listening Paper 3   58

    Solutions   70

Listening Paper 4   85

    Solutions   96

Oral (speaking) Primer   110

    Mark Scheme   110

    Analysis of Sample Conversation Recordings   115

    Example Questions   117

Steps To A Higher Grade   120

Topic Guide

The same core topics are tested by all exam boards, sometimes with slightly different titles (and often with a fair bit of crossover between the sub-topics listed below, depending on the board).

Home and Abroad

- ✓ Town and rural life
- ✓ Weather and climate
- ✓ Everyday life and traditions abroad
- ✓ Neighbourhood and region

- ✓ Holidays and tourism
- ✓ Services such as using the phone, bank or post office
- ✓ Travel, transport and directions

Education and Employment

- ✓ School life
- ✓ School routine
- ✓ Childhood

- ✓ Future plans
- ✓ Jobs and careers
- ✓ Ambitions: further study; volunteering

House, Home and Daily Routine

- ✓ Types of home
- ✓ Self, family, friends and relationships

- ✓ Household chores
- ✓ Food and drink

The Modern World and the Environment

- ✓ Technology and information e.g. internet, mobile phones, social media
- ✓ Environmental issues

- ✓ Current affairs and social issues
- ✓ The media e.g. TV, film, newspapers
- ✓ Bringing the world together: events, campaigns and good causes

Social Activities, Fitness and Health

- ✓ Hobbies, pastimes, sports and exercise
- ✓ Shopping and money

- ✓ Celebrations, customs and festivals
- ✓ Accidents, injuries and health issues

Listening Paper 1

Visit **rsleducational.co.uk/germanaudio** *to download the audio file for this paper.*

You may pause the recording between questions to allow yourself reading and writing time.

If you wish to complete this paper in timed conditions, allow a maximum of 45 minutes plus 5 minutes of reading time.

Instructions

- Use **black** ink or ballpoint pen.
- Answer **all** questions.
- Answer the questions in the spaces provided.
    - *There may be more space than you require.*
- Dictionaries are not allowed.

Advice

- You have 5 minutes to read through the paper before the recording starts.
- You will hear each extract twice. You may write at any time during the examination. There will be a pause after each question.
- Read each question **carefully** before attempting it.
- The marks available for each question are given in [square brackets]. These give you an indication of how long to spend on each question.
- There is a total of **50 marks** available for this paper.
- Leave time to check your answers at the end, if possible.

Answer ALL questions.

Michaels Rucksack

1   Was hat Michael in seinem Rucksack? Kreuzen Sie [X] die richtigen Antworten an.
        What does Michael have in his rucksack? Put a cross [X] by each correct answer.

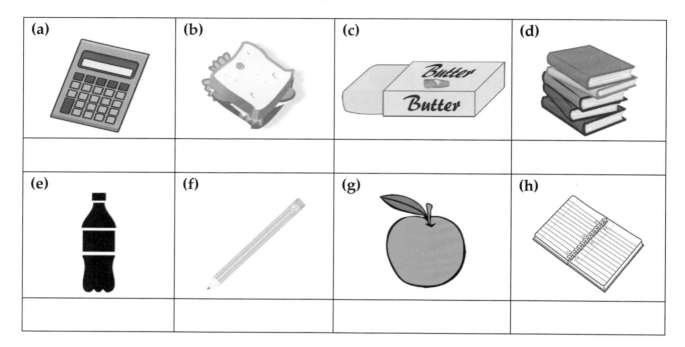

(Total for Question 1 = 4 marks)

Meine Stadt

2   Was machen diese Leute dieses Wochenende? Tragen Sie den richtigen Buchstaben
     in die Kästchen ein.

     Where are these people doing this weekend? Enter the correct letters in the boxes.

Beispiel: A
(a)
(b)
(c)
(d)
(e)

(Total for Question 2 = 5 marks)

Im Kino

3   Was sagen diese Leute über den Film? Kreuzen Sie **[X]** die richtigen Antworten an.
       What are these people saying about the film? Put a cross **[X]** by each correct answer.

(a) What time does the film start?

07:30	
08:30	
18:30	
19:30	

(b) What type of film is it?

Romantic	
Horror	
Action	
Comedy	

(c) When are they going to see a romantic film together?

Tonight	
Next Friday	
Next Saturday or Sunday	
Never	

(d) What does he also suggest?

Cook dinner	
Book a hotel	
Go to a restaurant	
Watch a football match	

(Total for Question 3 = 4 marks)

Meine Lieblingsfächer

4   Kreuzen Sie [X] die richtigen Kästchen an, um die entsprechende Zeit für diese Fächer zu zeigen: die **Vergangenheit**, die **Gegenwart** oder die **Zukunft**.

Put a cross [X] in each correct box to show the correct timeframe for these subjects: the **past**, the **present**, or the **future**.

	Vergangenheit	Gegenwart	Zukunft
Beispiel: Geography		X	
(a) German			
(b) English			
(c) Languages			
(d) Medicine			
(e) Maths			

(Total for Question 4 = 5 marks)

Mein Schulleben

5 Was denkt diese deutsche Studentin über ihre Schule? Kreuzen Sie [**X**] die fünf richtigen Antworten an.

What does this German student think of her school? Put crosses [**X**] by the **five** correct answers.

A Meine Schule ist ein großes Gymnasium.	**X**
B Es gibt viele Sportmannschaften.	
C Es gibt nicht genügend Lehrer an der Schule.	
D Ich mag die Schulbibliothek.	
E Ich spiele im Schulorchester.	
F Ich bin musikalisch begabt.	
G Es ist schwer, neue Freunde zu finden.	
H Ich habe keine Ahnung, was ich an der Uni studieren möchte.	
I Ich will im Ausland studieren.	
J Meine Mutter ist Lehrerin.	

(Total for Question 5 = 5 marks)

Suchst du ein neues Handy?

6   Hören Sie sich diese Werbung für eine Handyfirma an und kreuzen [X] die richtigen
Antworten an. Was sagt die Werbung?

Listen to this advertisement for a mobile phone company and put crosses [X] by the
correct answers. What does the advert say?

Beispiel This advert is for a new:

A mobile phone	X
B app	
C business idea	
D bank	

(a) The new phones are:

A slow	
B boring	
C cheap	
D expensive	

(b) Which service are we told is **free**?

A Sending messages	
B Connecting to the internet	
C Watching TV	
D Downloading music	

(c) What is special about the customer service? Cross **two** boxes.

A It is 24-hours.	
B There are never any problems.	
C It is the best in the world.	
D Their employees are highly trained.	
E There are never any queues or delays.	

(d) To register your interest:

A Phone the company.	
B Visit a local branch.	
C Visit the website.	
D Send an email.	

(Total for Question 6 = 5 marks)

Interview

7 Hören Sie sich dieses Interview mit einem Schriftsteller an und schreiben darunter Ihre Antworten auf die Fragen **auf Englisch**.

Listen to this interview with a writer and write your answers to the questions below **in English**.

(a) Why is the writer's next project different to his previous work? [1]

....

(b) How does he feel about it? Give **two** ideas. [2]

....

....

(c) What does he think about reviewers? Give **two** ideas. [2]

....

....

(d) Who is his biggest influence? [1]

....

(e) Why does he like reading children's books? Give **two** ideas. [2]

....

....

(Total for Question 7 = 8 marks)

Berufspraktikum

8   **Laura** zufolge, was waren die Vor- und Nachteile ihres Berufspraktikums?
*Antworten Sie **auf Deutsch** und in jedem Kästchen, aber schreiben Sie **nicht** in ganzen Sätzen!*

According to **Laura**, what were the advantages and disadvantages of her work experience placement?
*You should answer **in German** and in every box, but you do **not** have to write in full sentences.*

Vorteile

Beispiel: Um viele neue Leute kennenzulernen

Nachteile

(Total for Question 8 = 6 marks)

Helmut Schön – Bundestrainer*

9   Hören Sie sich diese Radiosendung an und wählen das treffendste Wort, um die Sätze fertigzustellen.

Listen to this radio broadcast and choose the most appropriate word to complete the sentences.

Beispiel: Helmut Schön war ~~NEUNZIG~~/**EINUNDACHTZIG** Jahre alt, als er starb.

(a) H. Schön ist einer der **ERFOLGREICHSTEN/BERÜHMTESTEN** Bundestrainer aller Zeiten.   [1]

(b) Seine **TOCHTER/TANTE** hat ein Radiointerview gegeben.   [1]

(c) Sie sagt, dass H. Schön von **ALLEN/NIEMANDEN** vermisst werden wird.   [1]

(d) Man hat ihn **VATI/PAPI** genannt.   [1]

(e) Viele deutsche Fußballfans haben **KARTEN/GESCHENKE** geschickt.   [1]

(f) In allen deutschen Stadien wird es eine Minute **STILLE/APPLAUS** geben.   [1]

(g) Große Bildschirme werden Schöns **GESICHT/LEISTUNGEN** zeigen.   [1]

(h) Die Stadien werden Gedenkmünzen und Kleidung **VERKAUFEN/KAUFEN**.   [1]

* *Bundestrainer* = German national football team coach

(Total for Question 9 = 8 marks)
TOTAL FOR PAPER 1 = 50 MARKS

Listening Paper 1 – SOLUTIONS

> On the audio track, the questions occur in quick succession. This is to avoid too many long pauses and move you on to the next question as efficiently as possible, as well as making it easy to find questions for those dipping in and out for practice. You may pause the track between each question.

Michaels Rucksack

> **1 Was hat Michael in seinem Rucksack?**
> *(b), (d), (e), (g)*   [4]

The first four or so questions in each of these papers are suitable for Foundation Level and Higher Level candidates. Questions such as these test simple core vocabulary.

You are required to put a cross to indicate which pictures correspond to the German words you hear in the recording. Check the marks at the bottom of the question: there are **four** marks available so make sure that you cross <u>exactly</u> four boxes!

> ### TOP TIP: Bring a pencil (and an eraser)!
>
> The **first time** you hear the recording, make notes in pencil. You can also put a mark (a cross or a dot) next to the answers you think are right (**not** in the answer box itself). Make sure to keep listening while you are doing this!
>
> You can also **cross out** each picture in pencil once you have used it, so you can see quickly and clearly which ones are left. Do this neatly, however, in case you make a mistake and need to repeat the question.
>
> The recording will then play a **second time**, giving you the chance to check your answers. There will be a short pause after the first recording, and again after the second time you hear it. Use this time to confirm the crosses you are confident about, and erase any that are incorrect.

The answers don't necessarily occur in the same order in the dialogue as in the pictures. Pay attention: in this recording, each answer is only mentioned once, and they come in quick succession. Michael mentions that his rucksack contains his lunch and then details exactly what his lunch is: a sandwich, a piece of fruit and a drink. He also adds that his schoolbooks (note: plural!) are in his bag too — **not** the single notebook shown in **(h)**!

Below is a transcript of the recording, with the key information given in **bold**.

Full Transcript:

*Jeden Morgen nehme ich meinen Rucksack, der mein Mittagessen enthält. Das heißt ein **Sandwich**, ein Stück **Obst** und ein **Getränk**. Ach ja, außerdem gibt es darin alle meine **Schulbücher** natürlich!*

Mark Scheme:

0-4	- Award one mark for each correct answer, up to four. - Deduct one mark for each incorrect answer, even if the correct answers are also crossed. *- Therefore, crossing eight boxes would mean four wrong answers, scoring 0 marks.*

Meine Stadt

2 Was machen diese Leute dieses Wochenende?	
(a) *B*	[1]
(b) *E*	[1]
(c) *G*	[1]
(d) *F*	[1]
(e) *C*	[1]

This question tests simple vocabulary in context: in this case, leisure activities and places. There are four marks available: one per correct answer. You will hear each person twice, including the example. Make sure to listen carefully as the examiner is likely to add common traps.

TOP TIP: Pay attention to the whole sentence.

Even if you don't know the meaning of the key word in the recording - or have forgotten it - keep listening to the rest of the sentence for clues and context. Another reason to listen carefully to the entire sentence is that a common mistake is to stop listening once you think you have heard the right answer. There may be traps!

For example, in **2(a)** the speaker says that he normally works in a restaurant … but he has this weekend off so he is going camping (**B**)! Hopefully you will have spotted this, but some more trigger-happy students will not have, because they will have heard the word *Restaurant* and rushed to select **C**.

In **2(b)**, the speaker says that she always goes with her father to the stadium to support the local football team. As there is no box for *Stadion*, the correct answer will have to be **E**: football.

The speaker in **2(c)** mentions a specific place - the park - for which there <u>is</u> a corresponding picture (**G**). He says that the activity they do there is *Tischfußball*: "<u>table</u> football", ruling out **E** as an answer.

There is also a trap in **2(d)**, although unlike in **2(a)**, the relevant information comes first: that she has to finish her homework (**F**). The fact that she wanted to go a concert instead (past tense!) is a red herring and irrelevant.

Finally, in **2(e)** he is going to a restaurant (for Italian food) with his girlfriend: **C**.

Full Transcript — Answers are given in **bold**, and <u>**traps**</u> are both <u>**underlined and bold**</u>:

Female: *Diesen Samstag habe ich gar keine Pläne… Jedoch will ich Sonntag mit meinen Freunden ins **Kino**.*
Male: *Normalerweise <u>**arbeite ich in einem französischen Restaurant**</u>, aber dieses Wochenende habe ich frei, deshalb gehe ich auf dem Land **Camping**.*
F: *Jedes Wochenende gehe ich mit meinem Vater zum **Stadion**, um die lokale Fußballmannschaft zu unterstützen.*
M: *Ich treffe meinen besten Freund im **Park**, wo wir immer **Tischfußball** spielen.*
F: *Ich muss meine **Hausaufgaben** fertig machen, aber <u>**ich wollte in ein Konzert gehen**</u>.*
M: *Ich gehe mit meiner Freundin in die Stadt zum **Abendessen**. Ich will italienisches Essen.*

Mark Scheme:

0-5	- Award one mark for each correct answer, up to five. - Incorrect answers do not score. Multiple answers score 0 marks for that question.

Im Kino

3 Was sagen diese Leute über den Film?	
(a) *18:30*	[1]
(b) *Action*	[1]
(c) *Next Saturday or Sunday*	[1]
(d) *Go to a restaurant*	[1]

The recording occurs as a dialogue. Multiple-choice questions such as this will often leave gaps between questions, as well as natural pauses, but this isn't guaranteed. Therefore, make sure you have read through the questions and possible answers in the allocated time <u>before</u> the recording starts.

As ever, listen out for both clues and traps. It is also a good idea, as you read the possible answers, to be thinking of key phrases and likely synonyms, as the recording may not give the exact word you are listening for.

TOP TIPS: Telling the time in German.

Just as in English, there are several ways of telling the time in German, and most of these have a direct English counterpart. For example, 1pm could be either *ein Uhr* or *dreizehn Uhr* (i.e. 13:00, using a 24-hour clock). Midnight can therefore be *null Uhr* or *vierundzwanzig Uhr*, or simply *Mitternacht*.

You could also state whether the given time is in the morning (*morgen[s]* or *früh*) or the evening (*abend[s]*) e.g. *Ich arbeite von acht Uhr morgens bis sechs Uhr abends* (= I work from 8am to 6pm). In the build-up to **3(a)**, for example, the male speaker makes it clear that he is talking about "this evening" (*heute abend*).

To express a precise number of minutes after or to the hour, you can simply state *Es ist achtzehn Uhr neun* (= 6:09pm) or use *nach* (after) or *vor* (before) e.g. *Es ist neun nach achtzehn*. Quarter past is therefore *Viertel nach…* and quarter to is *Viertel vor…*

However, the trickiest part to remember for native English-speakers (and therefore very commonly tested) is that ***halb acht* means "half past <u>seven</u>", NOT "half past eight"**. Think of it as "halfway to eight".

Therefore the answer to **Q3(a)** is 18:30, not 19:30.

Write out numbers.

It is a good idea, if you see a time or number in a Listening Paper, to write it out in full **before** the recording begins, so that you are prepared. This is especially true of difficult time phrases (e.g. *halb acht* = 7:30) and longer numbers (e.g. *achtundsechzig* = 68).

3(b) The next section of the dialogue mentions three of the four possible answers, which emphasises the need to listen carefully and in full. For instance, he says that it is ***kein*** (no/not a) horror film, but rather a gripping/exciting (*spannend*) film full of action and drama, which all points to the correct answer of an **Action** film. Silke then replies that this sounds terrible and she prefers romantic films, but that it doesn't matter.

3(c) They therefore come to a compromise that they will see a romantic film (*Liebesfilm*) next week, and Silke says she can only do the weekend, and can't make next Friday night. Therefore, the answer is **Next Saturday or Sunday**.

3(d) Finally, he suggests that before the film, they can go for dinner (*zum Abendessen gehen*). This suggests going to a restaurant, rather than staying in and cooking or ordering a takeaway. She agrees with emphasis: she hates cooking, and even suggests an excellent **restaurant** (*Gasthaus*) that she knows. There is also a potential trap, in that she says that this restaurant is near the football stadium.

TOP TIP: Learn synonyms (and antonyms).

As mentioned above, it is a useful tactic when learning vocabulary to group similar words together. It is unlikely that examiners will repeat the same language in the passage or recording that they have used in the question. For example, a question about a *Restaurant* may use the words *Gasthaus* or (*Speise*)*local*, or even a word like *Café*. By learning groups of synonyms you will be better prepared for these questions. You may also find that it increases your range of vocabulary in English!

Likewise, keep track of common antonyms, or words that have opposite meanings, so that you can avoid traps and red herrings. The answer to the question *Was mag er?* (What does he like?) might begin with the speaker saying *ich liebe…* (for example) but wouldn't begin *ich hasse…* , *es gefällt mir nicht*, or *ich kann es nicht leiden*, etc.

Full Transcript — Answers are given in **bold**, <u>clues</u> are <u>underlined</u>, and **<u>traps</u>** are both **<u>underlined and bold</u>**:

M: *Hey Silke, willst du gern heute <u>Abend</u> mit mir ins Kino?*
F: *Um wie viel Uhr?*
M: *Der Film, den ich sehen möchte, fängt um* **halb sieben** *an.*

F: *Was für ein Film ist das?*
M: *Es ist* **<u>kein Horrorfilm</u>**, *sondern ein <u>spannender</u> Film voller* **Action** <u>*und*</u> **Drama**.
F: *Das klingt schrecklich, aber macht nichts.* **<u>Ich schaue eigentlich nur Liebesfilme</u>**.

M: *Also wir können <u>nächste Woche</u> einen ansehen. Was sagst du dazu?*
F: *In Ordnung, aber es muss am* **Wochenende** *sein.* **<u>Nächsten Freitag kann ich nicht</u>**.

M: *Klingt gut. Wir können auch vorher* **Abendessen gehen**, *wenn dir das zusagt?*
F: *Na gut, da <u>ich nicht kochen will</u>, lass uns Essen gehen. Es gibt ein ausgezeichnetes <u>Gasthaus</u>* **<u>in der Nähe vom Fußballstadion</u>**. *Soll ich reservieren?*

Mark Scheme:

0-4	- Award one mark for each correct answer, up to four. - Incorrect answers do not score. Multiple answers score 0 marks for that question.

Meine Lieblingsfächer

4 Die Vergangenheit, die Gegenwart oder die Zukunft?	
(a) *Gegenwart*	[1]
(b) *Vergangenheit*	[1]
(c) *Vergangenheit*	[1]
(d) *Zukunft*	[1]
(e) *Zukunft*	[1]

This question asks whether the subjects mentioned belong to the past, present or future. In many cases, the tenses used in the recording will give you the biggest clue as to the timeframe in question, but some answers require a bit more attention.

Both the example and **(a)** are fairly straightforward: *studiere*, *ist*, and *bin* are all in the <u>present tense</u> and tell us what he is studying <u>now</u>. By contrast, he refers to English **(b)** in the past (*ich habe…studiert* and *war*).

(c) requires some careful listening and consideration because, although he refers to French in the present tense, he then says he has dropped it and now doesn't study any languages. Two potential pitfalls are hearing the word *jetzt* (now) and incorrectly ticking *Gegenwart*, or not understanding that he has dropped it (*abgewählt*). The key word is *keine*, showing that he doesn't study <u>any</u> languages, including French. We already know that he doesn't study English anymore.

He then says that he wants to be a doctor **(d)** when he is older (future), but his teacher says that this is not possible because he <u>didn't</u> take maths **(e)** last year. Therefore, he has to take an intensive maths course <u>next year</u> (future).

It's useful to **underline** and **translate key words** in the questions if you can, making use of the reading time at the start of the exam. When you listen to the recording, this will help you focus on the key information.

Full Transcript:

M: *Ich <u>studiere</u> viele verschiedene Fächer in der Schule, zum Beispiel **Erdkunde** und Biologie. Mein Lieblingsfach <u>ist</u> **Deutsch**, weil ich von der Literatur begeistert <u>bin</u>. Ich <u>habe</u> auch in der Vergangenheit **englische Literatur** <u>studiert</u>, Shakespeare zum Beispiel, aber es <u>war</u> sehr schwer. Das Schulfach, das ich am meisten hasse, ist <u>Französisch</u>. <u>Ich habe es abgewählt</u>, also <u>studiere ich jetzt</u> <u>**keine Fremdsprache** mehr</u>.*

*<u>Ich will</u> **Arzt** <u>werden</u>, wenn ich <u>älter</u> bin, aber der Lehrer sagt, dass das nicht möglich ist, weil ich letztes Jahr **Mathe** nicht studiert habe. Deshalb muss ich <u>nächstes Jahr</u> einen intensiven Kurs belegen, und erst dann kann ich die Mathe-Prüfungen mit dem Rest der Klasse machen.*

Mark Scheme:

0-5	- Award one mark for each correct answer, up to five. - Incorrect answers do not score. Multiple answers score 0 marks for that question.

Mein Schulleben

5 Was denkt diese deutsche Studentin über ihrer Schule?	
C, D, F, I, J	[5]

This question also refers to the topic of school and education, although with lots of crossover into sports and hobbies. You are required to pick out information from a slightly longer passage and compare it to the sentences. The question tells you that there are five correct sentences - one for each correct box ticked - not including the example: the five available marks make clear that the example is not one of the five answers requested. Check that there are exactly six answers crossed (including the example) when you have reached the end of the question.

The answers occur in order, which will help you to keep track. Listen out for key phrases used in the sentences and think of possible synonyms for the most important words, or other ways the recording could paraphrase the same meaning.

For example:

A *Meine Schule ist ein großes Gymnasium.*
= *"Meine Schule, das <u>ein Gymnasium mit vielen Studenten</u> ist"*.

However, **remember**: just because a word or two from one of the sentences is said in the recording, this does not mean that the whole sentence is automatically true. Take everything in its context, and make notes to review in the pause - there won't be enough time to do this while you're listening.

Sentence **B** - that there are many sports teams - isn't mentioned, although she does wish that there were more <u>types</u> of sporting activities, and then names a few sports. The reason for this is that there aren't enough members of staff (**C**). Instead, she enjoys spending lots of time in the library (**D**).

She then tells us that she plays the clarinet and <u>intends</u> (*vorhaben*) to join the school orchestra - in other words, she hasn't done this yet. Her music teacher thinks that she has a lot of talent (**F**, *musikalisch begabt*: musically gifted).

When she talks about going to university, she mentions that she wants to study music (so **H** is incorrect, because she knows what she wants to study) at a university in London, so **I** is correct (remember that London is abroad for this German student). Finally, she says that her mother hopes that she gets the same job as her. The speaker, however, does not want to teach children - which means that her mother is a teacher, and therefore **J** is correct!

Full Transcript:

F: *Meine Schule, das* <u>*ein Gymnasium mit vielen Studenten*</u> *ist, bietet viele Chancen an. Oftmals wünsche ich mir, dass es* <u>*mehr Sportarten*</u> *gäbe, das heißt Fußball, Tennis, Hockey und so weiter, aber der Direktor sagt mir, es sei unmöglich. Der Grund?* <u>*Es gibt einfach kein Personal*</u>*, um mehr Aktivitäten anzubieten. Deshalb verbringe ich* <u>*viel Zeit im Bibliotheksgebäude. Es gefällt mir sehr gut*</u>*, weil es immer ruhig und still ist. Nächstes Jahr will ich sozialer sein, zum Beispiel spiele ich gern Klarinette, also habe ich vor, nächstes Jahr Mitglied des Orchesters zu werden. Mein Musiklehrer denkt, das wäre eine sehr gute Idee, denn* <u>*ich habe viel Talent*</u> *und ich kann auf diese Weise viele ähnliche Leute kennenlernen. In der Zukunft will ich Musik an* <u>*einer Universität in London*</u> *studieren. Meine Mutter hofft, dass ich* <u>*denselben Job*</u> *wie sie bekomme, aber ich will keine* <u>*Kinder unterrichten.*</u>

Mark Scheme:

0-5	- Award one mark for each correct answer, up to five. - Deduct one mark for each error, even if correct answers are also crossed. - *Therefore, crossing ten boxes would mean five wrong answers, scoring 0 marks.*

Suchst du ein neues Handy?

6 Was sagt die Werbung?	
(a) *C*	[1]
(b) *A*	[1]
(c) *A, D*	[2]
(d) *C*	[1]

This advert about a new mobile phone (*Handy*) requires simple multiple-choice answers (in English) to test your comprehension of a much longer passage. Remember to listen out for synonyms and key phrases, as well as antonyms!

TOP TIP: Always read the question carefully

Don't rush into an answer as quickly as possible; it is vital to read the specifics of the question. There may be a trick word or a set of instructions that you hadn't expected. Sometimes this might be as simple as giving **two** pieces of information instead of one ... or it might be a potential trap. For example, **(a)** asks what quality of the **new** phones is mentioned, whereas the beginning of the recording mostly focuses on your old phone. In some cases, key words in the question are given in **bold**. You may find it helpful to <u>underline</u> other key words with a pen or pencil.

6(a) This question is a good example of the need to pay attention to the question, as well as the context given in the recording, because the advert asks if you are fed up (*die Nase voll haben*) with your old, slow phone that also costs a lot of money, before saying that the <u>new</u> products are totally the opposite! The answer is **C**, as it directly opposes the concept of slowness. Neither "boring" nor its antonym ("interesting") is mentioned.

6(b) This is another example of why you must pay attention to the specifics of the question: which service is <u>free</u>. Whilst almost all of the options are mentioned, only one is actually free.

Downloading music, films and TV, for example, we are told will cost <u>almost</u> nothing (*fast nichts*), whilst connecting to the internet will be *preiswert* and there are several *Billigangeboten* - in other words, things that are cheap but not completely free. Texting (the abbreviation *SMS* is given, as well as the full *Kurzmitteilung Service*) is, however, *kostenlos*. Therefore, the answer is **A**.

6(c) Hopefully you noticed that this question asks you to mark **two** boxes instead of one. Both bits of key information occur in the same sentence: that their team of experts (**D**) work night and day (**A**), and **D** is repeated when we are told that their employees must undergo an intensive training course. The recording also mentions that they can solve problems simultaneously all around the world, but whether this service is the best in the world is not mentioned.

6(d) Finally, the recording says that <u>before</u> you visit a local shop, you should arrange an appointment <u>online</u>, i.e. on the website (**C**).

Full Transcript:

M: *Suchst du ein neues Handy? Hast du die Nase voll von deinem alten, langsamen Handy, das auch <u>so viel Geld kostet</u>? Unsere Produkte sind total <u>das Gegenteil</u>! Man muss fast nichts dafür bezahlen, um Musik herunterzuladen oder Filme oder Fernsehsendungen zu sehen. Wir haben auch fantastische Billigangebote an 3G-Netz, anders gesagt wird es äußerst preiswert sein, im Internet zu surfen. Außerdem ist unser neuer Kurzmitteilungs-Service (das heißt SMS) <u>kostenlos</u>, und auch schneller und effektiver als die jetzigen Apps wie beispielsweise WhatsApp und Snapchat usw. [und so weiter].*

Wir wollen gerade eine neue Kundenservice Webseite für alle deine Sorgen und Klagen einführen. Unsere Mannschaft von <u>Experten</u> arbeitet <u>Tag und Nacht,</u> um deine Fragen so schnell wie möglich zu beantworten, auch wenn es viele andere Kunden gibt. Wir sind so stolz auf diesen Service, weil wir glauben, dass wir die einzige Firma sind, die gleichzeitig Probleme auf der ganzen Welt lösen kann. Unsere Arbeiter folgen einem <u>intensiven technischen Ausbildungskurs</u>, um alle unsere Produkte zu verstehen. Bevor du einen lokalen Laden besuchst, <u>musst du erst Online einen Termin ausmachen</u>.

Mark Scheme:

0-5	- Award one mark for each correct answer, up to five. - Incorrect answers do not score. Multiple answers score 0 marks for that question.

Interview

7(a) Why is the writer's next project different to his previous work? *- It is a stage (theatre) adaptation/play.* OR: *- He has never written for stage before.* [1]

Longer passages like this are designed to help the strongest candidates achieve top grades, and may contain unfamiliar words or terms. If you don't understand something that you hear, remember to listen to the context and try and work it out.

This section of dialogue occurs as one conversation, with no pauses until the end. Therefore, it's a good idea to make notes while listening to the recording. Unlike with multiple-choice questions, there is a danger of trying to write too much, meaning that you miss key information for the next question: be specific in answering, and don't just write down verbatim what is said. Writing down long sections of the dialogue is unwise, both because it is time-consuming and because it suggests to the examiner that you may not have understood the task.

TOP TIP: Make shorthand notes.

It is impossible to write everything down. Make abbreviated notes or only write down key words. For example, "he has never written for the stage before", is long, and by the time you've written that, the recording will have moved on. Writing something like "X stage b4" in the answer space allows you to quickly move on to the next question; you can return to it during the pauses or at the end of the listening section to write it out in full. Use the empty spaces on the question paper to make notes, but put your shorthand responses in the answer spaces to prevent you from from writing in the wrong section when you return to them.

The key piece of information to answer this question is that, unlike his previous work (mainly detective novels), his next piece is a theatrical adaptation. This is different because he has never written for the stage before.

*Mein kommendes Projekt ist auf einem meiner früheren Bücher basiert, also die gleichen Personen, die gleichen Themen, dieselbe Handlung usw., aber diesmal ist es eine **Theateradaption**. Ich bin sehr aufgeregt, weil ich noch nie <u>für die Bühne</u> geschrieben habe. Es wird wirklich ein Abenteuer sein!*

Remember to answer in English, as instructed! As a general rule, you should answer in the same language as the question - but do check the instructions at the top of the page.

7(b) How does he feel about it?
Any TWO of:
- *Excited/Exciting.* [1]
- *(It will be) An adventure.* [1]
- *He has never written for the stage before.* — NOT permitted for **both 7(a)** and **(b)**. [1]
[Maximum 2]

The same section of the recording as for **7(a)** gives you the information required to answer **7(b)**. The fact that he has never written for the stage before <u>is</u> acceptable as an answer provided that it isn't also your answer for **7(a)**. This is because it provides justification for his feelings of excitement (*aufgeregt*) or that it will be an adventure (*Abenteuer*).

7(c) What does he think about reviewers?
Any TWO of:
- *They have an important role.* [1]
- *He doesn't pay them any attention./He doesn't read reviews.* [1]
- *He doesn't want to be influenced by reviews.* [1]
[Maximum 2]

The key information for question **7(c)** is given in one long paragraph, and you are required to extract **two** correct pieces of information regarding his feelings for reviewers. You may give more, if you are unsure of one of your other points, but it might not be the best use of your time. Do make sure that your two points are different from each other.

The interviewer asks the writer what the reaction was like to his last book, and he interprets this as being about the critics' reviews:

Was die Kritiker angeht? <u>Gar keine Idee!</u> *Die Kritiker haben **eine wichtige Rolle**, aber als Künstler ist es auch lebensnotwendig, dass* <u>man sie überhaupt nicht beachtet</u>*. Das heißt, **ich lese nie die Rezensionen**, weil ich* <u>von ihnen nicht beeinflusst werden will</u>*.*

Some of this information overlaps, so it is important to separate your points. For example, the fact that he doesn't pay any attention to them and the fact that he never reads reviews are part of the same idea, as is the fact that he has no idea what the critical reaction to his last book was. However, you could add the justification that he doesn't read reviews <u>because</u> he doesn't want to be influenced by them; or state, on the other hand, that he says they play an important role.

7(d) Who is his biggest influence?
His (childhood/school) friends.   [1]

This is a slightly more straightforward question, as you aren't being asked to identify any reactions or opinions. However, you have to pay attention to the superlative in the question ("biggest"), because he does mention that he has many role models such as his colleagues and family, but especially (*hauptsächlich*) his childhood friends, whom he has known since (grammar) school. This is because they aren't interested in literature so he has to be humble and unpretentious around them! (This is an instance of some high-level vocabulary that you may not know, but this needn't stop you answering the question correctly.)

F: *Haben Sie Vorbilder?*
M: *Nicht wirklich. In Hinsicht auf meine Bücher; nicht besonders. Im Leben aber habe ich viele Rollenbilder, zum Beispiel meine Kollegen, meine Familie, und <u>hauptsächlich</u>* **meine Kindheitsfreunde**, *<u>die ich seit dem Gymnasium kenne</u>. Warum? Sie interessieren sich gar nicht für die Literatur! Also muss ich immer mit ihnen bescheiden und anspruchslos sein.*

7(e) Why does he like reading children's books?
Any TWO of:
- *The themes/characters are clear.*   [1]
- *One can learn a lot from children's authors/They are very disciplined.*   [1]
- *They are (often) short.*   [1]
- *He doesn't have to concentrate all the time (to follow the stories).*   [1]
                                                                                                   [Maximum 2]

The final question in this section is also worth two marks, so you need (at least) two pieces of information. The author says that he doesn't have time to read many different novels, but he does like reading children's books:

Ich habe heutzutage nicht genug Zeit, viele verschiedene Romane zu lesen, aber ich lese gern Kinderbücher, weil **die Themen und Personen klar sind**. *Man kann viel lernen, denn diese Art von Schriftstellern ist* **so diszipliniert**. *Außerdem sind sie oft* **kurz**, *und* **ich muss mich nicht ständig konzentrieren**, *um der Handlung folgen zu können.*

Any of the reasons he gives for liking children's books are acceptable as an answer, as long as they are distinct pieces of information. For example, "the themes and characters are clear" is really just the same idea (essentially, "things are clear"), so would only gain one mark. However, "they are short and so he doesn't have to concentrate continuously" would score two marks, because this point contains two distinct ideas.

Full Transcript:

F: *Erzählen Sie uns mehr über Ihre bevorstehende Arbeit.*

M: *Also normalerweise schreibe ich Romane, besonders Kriminalromane. Mein kommendes Projekt ist auf einem meiner früheren Bücher basiert, also die gleichen Personen, die gleichen Themen, dieselbe Handlung usw., aber diesmal ist es eine* **Theateradaption.** *Ich bin sehr* **aufgeregt,** *weil ich noch nie <u>für die Bühne</u> geschrieben habe. Es wird wirklich ein* **Abenteuer** *sein!*

F: *Prima! Wie war die Reaktion auf Ihr letztes Buch?*

M: *Was die Kritiker angeht? <u>Gar keine Idee!</u> Die Kritiker haben* **eine wichtige Rolle,** *aber als Künstler ist es auch lebensnotwendig, dass <u>man sie überhaupt nicht beachtet</u>. Das heißt,* **ich lese nie die Rezensionen,** *weil ich <u>von ihnen nicht beeinflusst werden will</u>.*

F: *Haben Sie Vorbilder?*

M: *Nicht wirklich. In Hinsicht auf meine Bücher; nicht besonders. Im Leben aber habe ich viele Rollenbilder, zum Beispiel meine Kollegen, meine Familie, und <u>hauptsächlich</u>* **meine Kindheitsfreunde,** *<u>die ich seit dem Gymnasium kenne</u>. Warum? Sie interessieren sich gar nicht für die Literatur! Also muss ich immer mit ihnen bescheiden und anspruchslos sein.*

Ich habe heutzutage nicht genug Zeit, viele verschiedene Romane zu lesen, aber ich lese gern Kinderbücher, weil **die Themen und Personen klar sind.** *Man kann viel lernen, denn diese Art von Schriftstellern ist* **so diszipliniert.** *Außerdem sind sie oft* **kurz,** *und* **ich muss mich nicht ständig konzentrieren,** *um der Handlung folgen zu können.*

Berufspraktikum

8 Laura zufolge, was waren die Vor- und Nachteile ihres Berufspraktikums? **Vorteile**	
- *Interessant* OR *Nicht langweilig/gelangweilt* OR *Viel zu tun.*	[1]
- *Viele Verantwortung* OR *Sie hat die Verantwortung genossen.*	[1]
- *Ihr(e) Chef/Kollegen (war(en) net) etc.* OR *(Sie ist) mit ihrem Chef/ihren Kollegen gut ausgekommen.*	[1]
Nachteile	
- *Ermüdend* OR *(Sie war sehr) müde*	[1]
- *(Sie musste) früh aufstehen.*	[1]
- *Die Kunden (klagen endlos)* OR *Sie konnte die Kunden nicht leiden.*	[1]

This is another long passage of dialogue, so the best method will be to make shorthand notes throughout and then fill the gaps in your notes during a pause. These final questions are designed to challenge the highest-scoring candidates, as a way of distinguishing between grades 8 and 9. In most cases, the question will be based on a fairly long recording, with written answers to test your comprehension (although some exam boards will have you answer in English rather than German). Make sure you know which board you are with and prepare accordingly!

You are listening for the positive and negative aspects of <u>Laura's</u> work experience, so don't mix this up with what Matthias says about his.

TOP TIP: Look for adjectives.

Listen out for adjectives and adverbs that have positive or negative connotations. For example, *wiederholend* and *langweilig* are negative (repetitive and boring) and describe Mathias's work experience, while Laura says that her experience was *genau das Gegenteil* (completely the opposite), although she didn't like the customers.

As this recording is in the form of a discussion, it is also a wise idea to pick-up where the **opinions** and **counter-arguments** are, which will help you decide which aspects are positive or negative. In this case, her experience is likely to have been the opposite of what Mathias says about his, because Laura says that hers was completely different.

Listen as best as you can, and try and piece the meaning together from the context. For example, if you don't know the verb *kennenlernen* (= to get to know) you might be able to understand that she met a lot of new people from *viele neue Leute*.

Positives and negatives don't necessarily occur in an ABAB order - there might be two negatives given in the same sentence. However, make sure that the reasons you give are different: *nicht langweilig* and *viel zu tun* make essentially the same point and so would only gain one mark.

Mark Scheme:

0-6	- Award one mark for each correct answer, up to six. There are three positive aspects, and three negative, and each must be in the correct section. - Each answer must contain clearly separate information or reasons, not repeat the same point in different words. - Incorrect or repeated answers do not score.

Full Transcript:

M: *Wie geht's, Laura? Du hast vor einem Monat dein Arbeitspraktikum gemacht, oder? Wie war's denn?*

F: *Hallo Matthias! Ja, wirklich gut. Ich habe ein Arbeitspraktikum ausgewählt, wo ich **viele neue Leute kennenlernen** konnte. Deshalb habe ich zwei Wochen in einem Supermarkt verbracht.*

M: *Oha, so lange! Warst du nicht sehr <u>müde und gelangweilt</u> danach?*

F: *Müde, ja natürlich, aber* **gelangweilt? Keine Chance!** *Ich hatte von Tag zu Tag so* <u>viel zu tun</u> *und* **ich habe die Verantwortung genossen.**

M: *Glück gehabt! Ich habe meinen Arbeitsplatz in einem Pflegeheim wiederholend und furchtbar langweilig gefunden. Außerdem waren meine Kollegen nicht sehr nett und ganz unhöflich.*

F: *Schade; für mich war es genau* <u>das Gegenteil</u>. **Ich bin besonders mit meinem Chef gut ausgekommen.** *Nützlich, als ich* **todmüde** *war, weil ich täglich* **sehr früh aufstehen musste.** *Er kaufte mir immer eine Tasse Kaffee vom Café im Supermarkt. Allerdings möchte ich keine Verkäuferin in der Zukunft sein, weil ich* **die Kunden nicht leiden konnte.** <u>Sie klagen endlos!</u>

Helmut Schön

9 (a) *erfolgreichsten*	[1]
(b) *Tochter*	[1]
(c) *allen*	[1]
(d) *Papi*	[1]
(e) *Karten*	[1]
(f) *Stille*	[1]
(g) *Leistungen*	[1]
(h) *verkaufen*	[1]

In this question, you are directed to choose **one** word in German to complete the sentence. The information occurs in order in the recording. Listen carefully, as the information may not be evenly distributed.

We are told for **9(a)** that Helmut Schön is the most successful German national coach to date, therefore the answer is *erfolgreichsten*. **(b)** asks who gave the radio interview about Helmut Schön: his daughter. **(c)** is looking for who Schön will be missed by – the agent of the passive verb *vermisst werden*. His daughter says that he will be missed by <u>everyone</u> (*von allen*). She goes on to say that is death is a tragedy, not just for the football world but for all of Germany. His nickname **(d)** is *Papi* becuase he was like a Father for German people. Question **(e)** wants to know what German football fans have sent Schön's family. They have sent *Beleidskarten* or *Kondolenzbriefen* ("sympathy cards" or "condolence letters"), therefore *Karten*. The answer to **(f)** is that there will be a minute's silence: *eine Minute Stille*, and the big screens **(g)** will show his achievements: *Leistungen*. The stadiums will sell (*verkaufen*) the clothing and commemorative coins **(g)**. Note that you don't have to understand *Gedenkmünzen* to be able to answer this question correctly. Don't focus on the words you don't know, but rather on what you **do** understand!

Mark Scheme:

0-8	- Award one mark for each correct answer, up to eight.
	- Incorrect answers do not score.

Full Transcript:

M: *Heute ist der 25. Jahrestag des Todestages des ehemaligen Managers von der deutschen Fussballnationalmannschaft Helmut Schön, der mit 81 Jahren starb. Schön ist **der bislang erfolgreichste Bundestrainer**, da er sowohl die Weltmeisterschaft, als auch die Europameisterschaft gewonnen hat. **Seine Tochter** hat in einem Interview mit der Radiostation Sport1 gesagt, dass wir eine schillernde Persönlichkeit verloren haben, **die von allen schmerzlich vermisst werden wird**:*

F: *"Sein Tod ist eine Tragödie nicht nur für die Fußballwelt, sondern auch für ganz Deutschland. **Sein Spitzname** —"Papi" — das ist für mich so passend, weil er wirklich wie ein Vater für alle Deutschen war. Ich habe schon so viele **Beileidskarten und Kondolenzbriefe** von Fussballfans deutschlandweit bekommen und das zeigt mir, dass er sehr beliebt war. Ich möchte ihnen jetzt "danke" sagen."*

F: *Es wird dieses Wochenende vor jedem Fussballspiel deutschlandweit **eine Minute Stille** geben, um den Jahrestag des Todestages von Herrn Schön zu gedenken. Während dieser Gedenkminute werden die **Leistungen** des ehemaligen Bundestrainers auf großen Bildschirmen im Stadion jeder Bundesligamannschaft gezeigt. Diese Stadien werden auch Gedenkmünzen, Trikots und andere Kleidungsstücke **verkaufen**, die Schöns Leben und Leistungen feiern.*

END OF SOLUTIONS FOR PAPER 1

Listening Paper 2

Visit **rsleducational.co.uk/germanaudio** to download the audio file for this paper.

You may pause the recording between questions to allow yourself reading and writing time.

If you wish to complete this paper in timed conditions, allow a maximum of 45 minutes plus 5 minutes of reading time.

Instructions

- Use **black** ink or ballpoint pen.
- Answer **all** questions.
- Answer the questions in the spaces provided.
  - *There may be more space than you require.*
- Dictionaries are not allowed.

Advice

- You have 5 minutes to read through the paper before the recording starts.
- You will hear each extract twice. You may write at any time during the examination. There will be a pause after each question.
- Read each question **carefully** before attempting it.
- The marks available for each question are given in [square brackets]. These give you an indication of how long to spend on each question.
- There is a total of **50 marks** available for this paper.
- Leave time to check your answers at the end, if possible.

Answer ALL questions.

Im Restaurant

1   Was bestellt Johannes? Kreuzen Sie [X] die richtigen Antworten an.
     What does Johannes order? Put a cross [X] in each correct box.

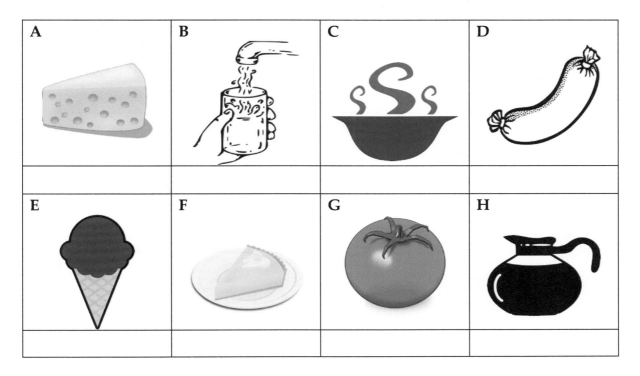

(Total for Question 1 = 4 marks)

Transport

2 Wie reist jede Person? Tragen Sie den richtigen Buchstaben in die Kästchen ein.
How does each person travel? Enter the correct letters in the boxes.

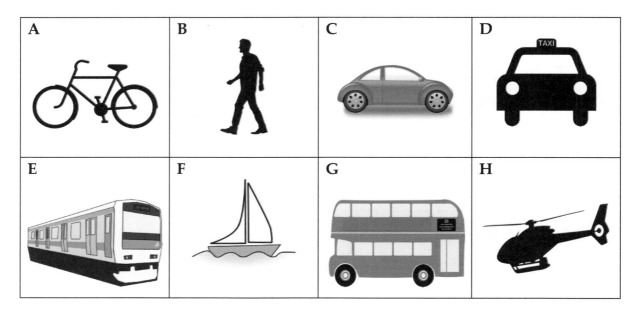

(a)	
(b)	
(c)	
(d)	

(Total for Question 2 = 4 marks)

Mein Schulleben

3   Was sagt Elke über ihr Schulleben? Wählen Sie den richtigen Buchstaben aus.
     What does Elke say about her school life? Choose the correct letter.

A zu Hause
B Mathe
C mit dem Bus
D Lehrerin
E lustig
F Ärztin
G Biologie
H langweilig
I zum Hockeyclub

(a) Die Lehrer sind ………..

(b) Ihr Lieblingsfach ist ………..

(c) In der Zukunft will sie ………. sein.

(d) Nach der Schule geht sie ………..

(Total for Question 3 = 4 marks)

Im Einkaufszentrum

4   Was kaufen diese Leute? Tragen Sie den richtigen Buchstaben in die Kästchen ein.
     What are these people buying? Enter the correct letters in the boxes.

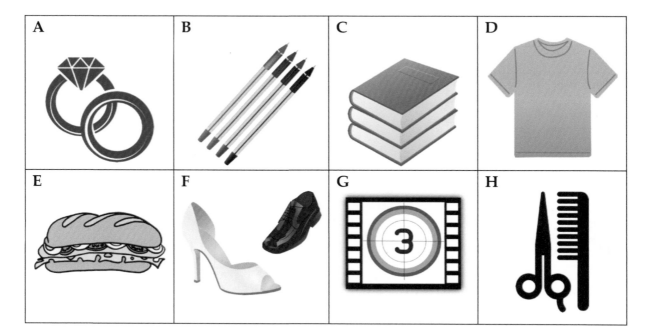

Beispeil C
(a)
(b)
(c)
(d)

(Total for Question 4 = 4 marks)

Wetterbericht

5 Wie ist das Wetter? Tragen Sie den richtigen Buchstaben in die Kästchen ein.
Einige Antworten erfordern mehr als einen Buchstaben und jeder Buchstabe kann mehr als einmal verwendet werden.

What is the weather like? Enter the correct letters in the boxes.
Some answers require more than one letter and each letter can be used more than once.

Beispiel: Monday	A	E
Tuesday		
Wednesday		
Thursday		
Friday		
Weekend		

(Total for Question 5 = 5 marks)

Fernsehsendungen

6   Was sagt Angela über Filme und Fernsehsendungen? Schreiben Sie **auf Englisch** die Antworten auf die Fragen.

What does Angela say about films and TV programmes? Answer the questions **in English**.

(a) The last time she saw a film was…

(i) Today	
(ii) Yesterday	
(iii) Last week	
(iv) More than a week ago	

(b) It was…

(i) A comedy	
(ii) A tragedy	
(iii) A drama	
(iv) A documentary	

(c) What does she watch **every day**?   [1]

....

(d) Why is it important not to watch too much TV? Give **one** idea.   [1]

....

(e) Why is this currently difficult for her?   [1]

....

(f) What does she think of televised football matches?   [1]

....

(Total for Question 6 = 6 marks)

Meine Familie und die Umwelt

7   Was macht Emres Familie, um die Umwelt zu schützen? Kreuzen Sie **[X]** die fünf richtigen Antworten an.

     What does Emre's family do to protect the environment? Put crosses **[X]** in the five correct boxes.

A Alle zur Schule radfahren	
B Taschen zum Supermarkt mitnehmen	
C Gemüse zu Hause kultivieren	
D Den Fernsehen ausmachen	
E Glasflaschen recyceln	
F Öffentliche Verkehrsmittel benutzen	
G Frisches Bio-Gemüse auf dem Markt kaufen	
H Energie zu Hause sparen	
I Duschen statt zu baden	
J Wasserflaschen nicht wegwerfen	

(Total for Question 7 = 5 marks)

Krankenhaus

8   Hören Sie sich diesen Bericht an und korrigieren die Sätze, indem Sie ein oder zwei
Wörter durchstreichen und ersetzen.

Listen to this report and correct the sentences by crossing out and replacing one or
two words.

(a) Das Krankenhaus liegt in Deutschland.

....   [1]

(b) Das Krankenhaus kümmert sich nur um Kinder.

....   [1]

(c) Karla ist Ärztin.

....   [1]

(d) Karla war in der Vergangenheit ungesund.

....   [1]

(e) Karla hat sechs Jahre lang auf der Straße gewohnt.

....   [1]

(f) Sie will allen Leuten helfen, die Familie haben.

....   [1]

(g) Die Grippe ist eine sehr seltene Krankheit unter den Patienten.

....   [1]

(h) Halsschmerzen sind das einzige Problem, die das Krankenhaus nicht behandeln kann.

……………………………………………………… [1]

(i) Das Krankenhaus bekommt Geld von der Regierung.

……………………………………………………… [1]

(j) Das Krankenhaus ist nach Karlas Tochter so benannt.

……………………………………………………… [1]

(Total for Question 8 = 10 marks)

Im Ausland studieren

9 (a) Hören Sie sich dieses Gespräch zwischen Freunden an. Was sind die Gründe dafür und dagegen, im Ausland zu studieren?

*Sie sollen **auf Deutsch** und in jedem Kästchen antworten, aber Sie müssen **nicht** in ganzen Sätzen schreiben.*

Listen to this conversation between friends. What are the reasons for and against studying abroad?

*You should write **in German** and in every box, but you **don't** have to write in full sentences.*

Dafür

Beispiel: Das Wetter ist besser.

Dagegen

[6]

(b) Nach Peters Lehrer, welche zwei **europäischen** Länder sind die besten, wenn er im Ausland studieren möchte? [2]

....

....

(Total for Question 9 = 8 marks)
TOTAL FOR PAPER 2 = 50 MARKS

Blank Page

Listening Paper 2 - SOLUTIONS

Im Restaurant

1 Was bestellt Johannes?	
C, D, F, H	[4]

Don't write/guess too early! The answers won't necessarily occur in the same order as the pictures, and there are even some items mentioned that don't have a corresponding picture.

Firstly, we hear the speaker ask what the soup of the day is, and he then confirms that it is tomato soup - so tick the box next to soup (**C**) and **not** tomatoes (**G**)! He then orders sausage - **D** - (and chips, but there isn't a box for chips!) followed by a slice of cheesecake (**F**) - <u>without</u> ice cream. Finally he wants a coffee (made with very hot water): the final box to cross is **H**, not **B**!

Mark Scheme:

0-4	- Award one mark for each correct answer, up to four.
	- Incorrect answers do not score. Multiple answers score 0 marks for that question.

Full Transcript – correct answers are given in **bold**:

M: *Bitte, was ist die* **Tagessuppe**? *Tomaten? Prima! Und danach möchte ich eine* **Wurst** *mit Pommes. Zum Dessert hätte ich gern ein Stück* **Käsekuchen**, *aber ohne Eis. Und ich trinke auch gern* **Kaffee** *mit extrem heißem Wasser. Danke schön!*

Transport

2 Wie reist jede Person?	
(a) *A*	[1]
(b) *B*	[1]
(c) *G*	[1]
(d) *D*	[1]

If you change your mind, erase or put a neat line through the wrong answer (e.g. ~~A~~), to signal to the examiner that you have changed your mind. Never leave multiple answers where only one is permitted.

Use the pause before the recording to think of words that are likely to match the pictures. For example, to go by car (or drive) could involve *das Auto* or *den Wagen*, and the verbs *nehmen* or *fahren*.

The answer to **2(a)** is fairly straightforward, as the speaker says that she travels by bike (**A**), even when it rains. Don't be thrown by this extra piece of (irrelevant) information. **2(b)** tries to catch you out by mentioning public transport, but he says he is scared of (*Angst haben vor*) it, and therefore prefers to walk (**B**). There is a similar trick in **2(c)**, because the speaker says that her parents <u>never</u> like to take the car: therefore she has to go by bus (**G**), which she doesn't like (*leider* = "unfortunately"). Some more trigger-happy students may just hear the word *Auto* and incorrectly write **C**. Finally, the speaker in **2(d)** says that he has broken his leg and therefore can neither walk (*zu Fuß gehen* is synonymous with *spazieren gehen*) nor drive a car. He has to pay a taxi driver when he wants to go into town (**D**).

Mark Scheme:

| 0-4 | - Award one mark for each correct answer, up to four. |
| | - Incorrect answers do not score. Multiple answers score 0 marks for that question. |

Full Transcript - answers are **bold**:

F: *Ich fahre jeden Tag mit dem **Rad**, auch wenn es regnet.*

M: *Ich habe Angst vor den öffentlichen Verkehrsmitteln und sowieso gehe ich lieber **spazieren**.*

F: *Meine Eltern wollen das Auto nie benutzen. Das heißt ich muss leider mit dem **Bus** fahren.*

M: *Ich habe mir das Bein gebrochen, also kann ich weder zu Fuß gehen noch mit dem Auto fahren.* ***Ich muss einen Taxifahrer bezahlen**, wenn ich in die Stadt gehen will.*

Mein Schulleben

3 Was sagt Elke über ihr Schulleben?	
(a) *E*	[1]
(b) *G*	[1]
(c) *F*	[1]
(d) *A*	[1]

This recording occurs without pauses, so you need to listen attentively throughout and extract the relevant information when it appears. The answers are not always obvious, but they do at least occur in order. With questions like this, you can often narrow down your choices to two or three before the recording has even started!

TOP TIP: Find the possible answers first.

When a question offers several words to complete a sentence, you can apply logic to eliminate the majority of the options before you have even heard the recording. Look at what would make sense in the context of the sentence. Is it missing a verb or a noun? An adjective or an adverb? If a verb is missing, which person (I, you singular, he/she/it, we, you plural, they)? If it's a noun, what type of noun? Could it be singular, plural, masculine, or feminine? You will then be left with only two or three options for each question.

In the case of **3(a)**, the sentence will conclude with a word or phrase to describe the teachers, so you are looking for an adjective, an adverbial phrase or a plural noun. There aren't any plural nouns here (*Lehrerin* and *Ärztin* are both <u>feminine singular</u>), and it is also unlikely that her teachers are at home (*zu Hause*). Realistically, you are left with two contrasting adjectives: *langweilig* and *lustig*. The recording says that the teachers are always funny, and *komisch* is synonymous with *lustig*, so the answer is **E**!

The possible answers for **3(b)** are even more limited, as we are looking for a school subject: therefore *Mathe* or *Biologie*. The previous sentence stated that the teachers are even funny in maths, which she doesn't find interesting, but it is worth listening to the next phrase, revealing that she prefers natural sciences. Therefore **G**, *Biologie*, is the only possible answer.

She goes on to say that she wants to study medicine. We can therefore infer that she wants to be a doctor (**F** *Ärztin*), which is the answer to **3(c)**. Finally, only the adverbial phrases *A*, *C*, and *I* fit for **Question 3(d)** and she says she likes <u>watching</u> sport <u>on the TV</u> with her parents. To do this, she is most likely to be at home (**A**).

Mark Scheme:

0-4	- Award one mark for each correct answer, up to four. - Incorrect answers do not score. Multiple answers score 0 marks for that question.

Full Transcript:

F: *Die Lehrer an meiner Schule sind immer **komisch**, auch in Mathe, das ich nicht interessant finde. Ich studiere am liebsten **Naturwissenschaften**. Die Lehrerin sagt, dass ich viel arbeiten muss, wenn ich **Medizin** studieren will. Nachdem der Unterricht zu Ende ist, schaue ich gern Sport **im Fernsehen mit meinen Eltern**.*

Im Einkaufszentrum

4 Was kaufen diese Leute?	
(a*)* *B*	[1]
(b) *A*	[1]
(c) *E*	[1]
(d) *F*	[1]

This is a seemingly straightforward question, which tests your shopping vocabulary, but of course remember to <u>listen to each sentence in full</u>, making notes if necessary, and to watch out for synonyms and traps! You can cross out a picture once you are sure of that answer, to help you narrow down the remaining choices.

The **example** states explicitly that the speaker wants to buy <u>books</u> (**C**) from the shopping centre. The next speaker **(a)** says that he will join her, as he needs pens (**B**) and pencils. The following question **(b)** is a good example of less obvious vocabulary **and** of a trap. She tells us that there is a *Juweliergeschäft* (a jewellery store) opposite the cinema. The answer is **A** - the cinema is mentioned at the last second as a trap! The next speaker **(c)** says that he is hungry, and they can meet up after he has eaten. He doesn't mention a specific food, but **E** is the only possible option for this question. The final speaker **(d)** says that she wants to go into the clothes store to buy <u>shoes</u> (**F**) - not clothes! It has nothing to do with school (**B** or **C**), although she wants to wear the shoes when she meets her school friends.

TOP TIP: Revise higher tier topic vocabulary!

Be ready for vocabulary that may need some thought, and don't listen out too fixedly for a word that you expect to hear. For example, knowing *eine Halskette* (necklace) and *Ringe* (rings) allows you to understand the word *Juweliergeschäft*, even if you did not previously know this.

Likewise, you may be listening out for the word *Sandwich* or *Butterbrot*, but the recording doesn't mention a specific type of food, just that he will eat something.

Mark Scheme:

0-4	- Award one mark for each correct answer, up to four.
	- Incorrect answers do not score. Multiple answers score 0 marks for that question.

Full Transcript:

F: *Ich muss ins Einkaufszentrum gehen, weil ich Bücher kaufen will. Und du, Vati?*
M: *Ich gehe mit dir. Ich brauche **Bleistifte und Kugelschreiber.***

F: *Ich will **eine Halskette und Ringe** kaufen. Es gibt ein gutes <u>Juweliergeschäft</u> gegenüber vom Kino.*

M: *Ich brauche nichts, aber ich habe doch **Hunger**. Wir können uns wieder treffen, nachdem ich etwas **gegessen** habe.*

F: *Ich möchte ins Kleidungsgeschäft gehen. Sie verkaufen sehr billige und modische **Schuhe**, die ich nächste Woche mit meinen Schulfreundinnen tragen will.*

Wetterbericht

5 Wie ist das Wetter?	
Tuesday *D*	[1]
Wednesday *B* (optionally also *D*)	[1]
Thursday *F*	[1]
Friday *A H*	[1]
Weekend *H*	[1]

There are many key areas of vocabulary that GCSE candidates neglect, and weather is often one of them! This exercise is trickier than it appears at first glance, and therefore represents a step-up in difficulty from the previous question. This is because - as the instructions at the top of the page state - some answers require more than one letter, and the letters may be used more than once. **Always read the instructions!**

Therefore, the advice that is given for some of the earlier questions - to cross out each answer once you have used it - is **not** relevant here.

Do make sure you have read the question and options first. Also, think of synonyms for each weather condition, as the recording is unlikely to repeat key vocabulary.

There is one mark per **fully correct** answer – some require two letters. Half-correct answers don't score, so make sure to listen closely to the entire sentence.

The example question clearly states that Monday will be hot and sunny - therefore the answer must be **A** and **E**. For Tuesday, however, we are told that it is no longer sunny (*keine Sonne mehr*) but rather cloudy (**D**). *Sondern* is a useful word, meaning "but rather". Even if you don't know the word *Wolke* (cloud), knowing that it is not sunny any more should narrow down your options!

Wednesday's report also says that it will be cloudy (*wolkig = viele Wolken*), but he also says that in the afternoon it will rain. Despite the use of *aber* these aren't contradictory ideas, but rather both **B** and **D** are correct - remember that answers can be used more than once! As the picture for **B** includes a cloud, this will be accepted by itself. The speaker then tells you to watch out on Thursday because there could be a storm (*Gewitter*). Therefore, **F** is the only appropriate answer.

Friday's report says that the sun will shine once again, but it will still be chilly - therefore **A** and **H** are both correct. The weekend will also be cold (**H** again), but with <u>no</u> chance of snow, so **C** is wrong.

Mark Scheme:

0-5	- Award one mark for each correct answer, up to five. - Incorrect answers do not score. Half-correct answers, or answers with surplus letters, also score 0 marks for that question. - *Therefore, if the candidate has given an incorrect answer **as well as** the correct answer, 0 marks are awarded for that question.*

Full Transcript:

M: *Und jetzt die Wettervorhersage für diese Woche. Am Montag ist es heiß und sonnig.*
*Am Dienstag gibt es aber keine Sonne mehr, sondern viele **Wolken**.*
*Am Mittwoch wird es auch **wolkig** sein, aber es wird am Nachmittag **regnen**.*
*Am Donnerstag könnte es ein **Gewitter** geben, also pass auf!*
*Am Freitag scheint die **Sonne** noch einmal, aber es ist noch **frostig**.*
*Am Samstag und Sonntag ist es auch **kalt**, aber ohne Chance auf Schnee.*

Fernsehsendungen

6 Was sagt Angela über Filme und Fernsehsendungen?	
(a) *(iv) More than a week ago*	[1]
(b) *(iii) A drama*	[1]
(c) *The news*	[1]
(d) EITHER:	
- One becomes <u>lazy</u>	
OR:	
- <u>Unhealthy</u>.	[1]
(e) *She has a TV in her room.*	[1]
(f) *Boring/She doesn't watch them*	[1]

This question combines multiple-choice questions with short responses in English, so make sure you are alert to the kind of response that is being asked of you. Giving yourself time to read the question will go a long way to helping you be prepared for this. It may help if you make notes during your reading time and/or when listening to the recording – see also *TOP TIP: Make shorthand notes* in **Listening Paper 1, Question 7(a)**.

TOP TIP: Make good use of the five minutes before the exam starts.

Because **the speed picks up** through these exercises, it is very important that you spend time reading the questions in the five minutes given to you at the start of the paper. That will allow you to follow the recordings more easily and look out for the key information. It is a good idea to **start at the back of the paper**, so you prepare for the most difficult questions first.

In **6(a)**, the information in the recording tells you that that she watched a film three weeks ago. The only appropriate answer is **(iv) More than a week ago**, even though she remembers it as if it were yesterday. She also says that, even though she laughed a lot, it wasn't a comedy, but a detective drama - therefore the answer to **Question 6(b)** has to be **(iii)**.

From **6(c)** onwards, the answers require short sentences or one-word answers. She actually mentions a variety of different types of programmes that she watches, but the question asks what she watches <u>every day</u> and she explicitly says this is the news (*die Nachrichten*). Always listen carefully for the exact piece of information that you need.

6(d) asks for one reason why you shouldn't watch too much TV and the speaker says one could become lazy and unhealthy. Either of these words would suffice to gain the mark here. She goes on to say that it is difficult for her to avoid temptation at the moment, as she has a TV in her room now. This is the answer to **6(e)**.

Finally, **6(f)** asks for her opinion of football matches on TV. Although she likes <u>playing</u>, she thinks these televised matches are boring. She does, however, say that she watches Formula 1 (*Formel Eins*) as often as possible because she likes the competition between the drivers.

Mark Scheme [6(a)-(b)]:

0-2	- Award one mark for each correct multiple-choice answer, up to two. - Incorrect answers do not score. Multiple answers score 0 marks for that question.

Mark Scheme [6(c)-(f)]:

0-4	- Award one mark for each correct answer, up to four. - Answers must be in English. Incorrect answers, or answers in German - or any other language - do not score. - Longer answers may be accepted, but too much extraneous information must result in 0 marks for that question, as it may imply that the candidate has not understood the task and has lifted indiscriminately.

Full Transcript:

*F: Ich habe **vor drei Wochen** einen Film gesehen, aber ich erinnere mich daran, <u>**als wäre es gestern gewesen**</u>. Ich habe viel gelacht, obwohl es ein **Polizeidrama** sein sollte und **keine Komödie**. Normalerweise schaue ich gern Dokumentarfilme, aber dieser Film war echt gut. Ich arbeite zu Hause, deshalb schaue ich viele verschiedene Sendungen, zum Beispiel Seifenopern, Quizsendungen und so weiter. Ich sehe <u>jeden Tag</u> die **Nachrichten** und es gibt manchmal einen guten Film, aber nicht sehr oft. Es ist wichtig, dass ich den Fernseher nicht so oft einschalte, weil **man faul und ungesund wird**. Es ist aber zur Zeit nicht so leicht, der Versuchung zu entgehen, da **ich seit einem Monat einen Fernseher in meinem eigenen Zimmer habe**. Ich spiele gern Fußball mit meinen Freunden, aber ich finde die im Fernsehen gezeigten Fußballspiele sehr langweilig, im Gegensatz zur **Formel 1**, die ich <u>so oft wie möglich</u> sehe, weil ich die Konkurrenz zwischen den Fahrern mag.*

Meine Familie und die Umwelt

7 Was macht Emres Familie, um die Umwelt zu schützen?   *B, C, F, H, J*   [5]

The techniques required here will test your ability to understand specific vocabulary - Recycling and the Environment - in context. There are five correct answers, and they don't occur in the same order in the recording! Remember to read the options carefully **before** the recording starts, so that you have an idea of what to listen out for, whilst also being mindful of possible synonyms or alternative ways of expressing the same concept.

For example, the first set of ideas about helping the environment overlap and you have to listen carefully to the entire section before selecting the correct answer:

*…wir benutzen unseren Wagen so selten wie möglich. Viel gesünder ist es, mit dem Rad zu fahren, aber meine Schwester ist noch zu jung dafür, also müssen wir alle **mit den öffentlichen Verkehrsmitteln** zur Schule fahren.*

The key pieces of information occur one after the other to give you the correct answer. To understand how to get there, you need to listen carefully. The speaker says that it would be healthy ("healthier") to ride a bike, but his sister is too young - you are teased with the possibility of option **A**, before being told that this is wrong. They all travel by public transport: **F**.

TOP TIP: Listen in chunks   It's often the case when learning languages that we try and understand every individual word when reading or listening; but a much better, more natural approach is to think in chunks. Therefore, listen to the whole sentence and listen out for clues and words you **do** understand, but don't get frustrated or preoccupied by the ones you don't. After a while you'll be able to focus on the meaning of the whole idea, rather than the individual words.

The next section of the recording expresses the idea that he refills his water bottle at school. The (double) use of *wieder* emphasises the idea of <u>re</u>-using his bottle, not throwing it away - so option **J** is correct. Option **E** refers to recycling glass bottles, and so is incorrect.

> *Wenn ich in der Schule bin, **fülle ich meine Flasche wieder mit Wasser auf**, weil es umweltfreundlicher ist, sie jeden Tag wieder zu verwenden.*

The next answer is also fairly straightforward, as he simply says to turn the lights off at home (*das Licht ausmachen*), when they aren't necessary. The word *ausmachen* <u>is</u> used in one of the options (**D**), but refers specifically to the television and not the lights. Therefore you want the more general option **H**, which relates to saving energy at home.

The next section is a little more obscure, but the speaker gives a lot of context to help you get the correct answers:

> *Beim Einkaufen kaufen wir keine Plastiktüten, weil sie nicht wiederverwendbar sind. Stattdessen **haben wir unsere eigenen Taschen**, die wir immer wieder benutzen. Aber wir müssen kein Gemüse im Supermarkt kaufen, weil **wir einen Gemüsegarten haben**, und wir bauen genug Bohnen und Karotten an, um sie auch den Nachbarn geben zu können.*

In other words, his family don't buy plastic bags when they are shopping, but use their own - so you need option **B**. They also don't buy vegetables in the supermarket, because they have their own vegetable garden: option **C**. Option **G** is a red herring.

Mark Scheme:

0-5	- Award one mark for each correct answer, up to five. - Deduct one mark for each incorrect answer, even if the correct answers are also crossed. *Therefore, crossing ten boxes would mean five wrong answers, scoring 0 marks.*

Full Transcript:

M: *Meine Familie und ich tun, was wir können, um der Umwelt zu helfen. Das heißt wir benutzen unseren Wagen so selten wie möglich. Viel gesünder ist es, mit dem Rad zu fahren, aber meine Schwester ist noch zu jung, also müssen wir alle **mit den öffentlichen Verkehrsmitteln** zur Schule fahren. Wenn ich in der Schule bin, **fülle ich meine Flasche wieder mit Wasser auf**, weil es umweltfreundlicher ist, sie jeden Tag wieder zu verwenden. Zu Hause müssen wir immer **das Licht ausmachen**, wenn es nicht mehr benötigt wird. Beim Einkaufen kaufen wir keine Plastiktüten, weil sie nicht wiederverwendbar sind. Stattdessen **haben wir unsere eigenen Taschen**, die wir immer wieder benutzen. Aber wir müssen kein Gemüse im Supermarkt kaufen, weil **wir einen Gemüsegarten haben**, und wir bauen genug Bohnen und Karotten an, um sie auch den Nachbarn geben zu können.*

Krankenhaus

8
(a) ~~Deutschland~~ → *Österreich/Wien*
(b) ~~Kinder~~ → *Bettler/Obdachlose*
(c) ~~Ärztin~~→ *(Medizin)Studentin*
(d) ~~ungesund~~ → *obdachlos*
(e) ~~Jahre~~ → *Monate*
(f) ~~Familie~~ → *Probleme*
(g) ~~seltene~~ → *häufige*
(h) ~~Halsschmerzen~~ → *Zahnschmerzen*
(i) ~~der Regierung~~ → *Freunden/Fremden/Spenden*
(j) ~~Tochter~~ → *Mutter*

Question 8 is aimed at Higher Tier students and requires corrections to the sentences provided (one or two words). Read the sentences first to make sure you understand and then compare them to the recording.

Be specific when you answer and only provide **one** correction to each sentence.

The hospital is in the <u>Austrian</u> capital, not in Germany. Either *Österreich* or *Wien* (not the English spelling "Vienna"!) would get you the mark for **8(a)**. The hospital doesn't focus on children (**8(a)**), but rather beggars (*Bettler*) or homeless people (*Obdachlose*).

TOP TIP: Write out words you don't know.

Get used to working out words that you don't know when you hear them. Write them down as accurately as you can on a spare bit of the page, and see if they look similar to another word, either in German or in English: they may share a common root, as English contains many words of German origin. Or maybe you can work out the meaning of the word from its individual components.

For example, *obdachlos* means "homeless". The suffix *-los* means "without" (or "less") and *Obdach* is a "shelter". *Dach* means "roof", and *ob* can mean "above"; therefore the whole word literally means "without a roof above".

Karla Moratti isn't a doctor (yet) – she is a *Medizinsstudentin*. Either the full word, or simply *Studentin* would get you the mark for **8(c)**. **8(d)** is in the imperfect tense (*war*) and explicitly asks what she used to be *in der Vergangenheit* and the recording says she is a "former homeless person" (*ehemalige **Obdachlose***). She lived on the street (**8(e)**) for six months, not years – don't be put off by the mention of *drei Jahren*. Now she wants to help people with <u>problems</u> (**8(f)**), not with families. She goes on to say that the flu (*die Grippe*) is one of the most common (*häufig* not *selten*) illnesses (**8(g)**), along with stomachache and a sore throat (*Halsschmerzen* in **8(h)**). The only disease they can't treat is toothache (*Zahnschmerzen*) and they have to call a dentist. The hospital receives charitable donations from friends and strangers (*wohltätige **Spenden von Freunden und Fremden***), not the government or local council. Either *Freunden* or *Fremden* (or both) is correct for **8(i)**. Finally, for **8(j)**, the hospital is named after Karla's late <u>mother</u>, not her daughter – you don't need to know that *selig* means "deceased" to get the mark!

Mark Scheme:

0-10	- Award one mark for each correct answer, up to ten. - Answer must indicate both the deleted word **and** the new word. - Incorrect answers do not score. - Misspelt answers are acceptable if the intended word is clearly understood.

Full Transcript:

M: *In **der österreichischen Hauptstadt Wien** gibt es ein Krankenhaus mit einem großen Unterschied: die Patienten sind alle **Obdachlose**. Das Wohltätigkeitsprojekt, das sich nur um Bettler kümmert, ist die Idee der **Medizinstudentin** Karla Moratti. Karla ist auch ehemalige **Obdachlose** und sie glaubt, deine Lebensverhältnisse sollten nichts mit deinen Gesundheitschancen zu tun haben.*

F: *Meine Mutti ist vor drei Jahren gestorben und ich konnte die Miete nicht alleine bezahlen. Ich habe **sechs Monate** auf der Straße gelebt, einschließlich Weihnachten. Das kann doch jedem passieren. Ich will allen helfen, wenn sie **Probleme** haben. Unsere Patienten haben verschiedene Krankheiten, aber die **häufigsten** sind: die Grippe, Magenschmerzen oder Halsschmerzen… Das einzige Problem, das wir nicht behandeln können, ist **Zahnschmerzen**. Dafür müssen wir einen hochspezialisierten Zahnarzt anrufen.*

M: *Karla hat dem Gemeinderat und der Regierung geschrieben, um Geld zu erbitten, aber für den Moment muss das Krankenhaus auf wohltätige **Spenden von Freunden und Fremden** vertrauen, um zu überleben. In der Zukunft wird es hoffentlich viele ähnliche Projekte weltweit geben. Eines steht aber fest: das Margarethe Moratti Krankenhaus - Karla hat es **nach ihrer seligen Mutter benannt** - ist das Erste und Einzige seiner Art.*

Im Ausland studieren

9(a) Was sind die Gründe dafür und dagegen, im Ausland zu studieren?

Answers may occur in any order, but must be in correct section. Paraphrasing and/or using these points in a sentence is acceptable, but incomplete sentences are also fine.

Dafür

In any order:

- *Kostenloses Studium*   [1]
- *Bessere Chancen auf dem (globalen) Arbeitsmarkt /Arbeitsgelegenheiten* etc.   [1]
- *Neue/Mögliche Freunde/Kontakte/Geschäftspartner*   [1]

Dagegen

In any order:

- *Deutsche Universitäten sind (weltweit) respektiert*   [1]
- *Heimweh*   [1]
- *Kulturelle Unterschiede*   [1]

[Maximum 6]

As we have seen in **Listening Paper 1**, the best method for extracting information from longer passages is to make shorthand notes throughout and then fill the gaps in your notes during a pause – see *TOP TIP: Make shorthand notes* in **Listening Paper 1, Question 7(a)**. This is especially the case when the answers occur very close together in the recording.

You are listening for reasons to study abroad and for reasons not to, according to the two speakers. Remember, you don't have to understand every word that is said. Try and piece the meaning together from the context (see *TOP TIP: Look for adjectives* in **Listening Paper 1, Question 8** and *TOP TIP: Listen in chunks* in **Listening Paper 2, Question 7**).

Remember that the reasons and counter-arguments for each side don't necessarily occur in an ABAB order, or even from the speaker you would expect. Use your judgement and make sure that the reasons you give are written in the correct column, as well as being different from each other. For example, the female speaker's argument that you can meet many new friends and business partners is <u>one</u> point; you don't get a mark for "friends" and another mark for "business partners".

See the full transcript below to check where the relevant information occurs in the recording. Remember that you don't have to write full sentences; just give the key words or phrases.

Mark Scheme 9(a):

0-6	- Award one mark for each correct answer, up to six. There are three positive aspects, and three negative, and they must be in the correct section. - Each answer must contain clearly separate information or reasons, not repeat the same point in different words. - Incorrect or repeated answers do not score.

9(b) Nach Peters Lehrer, welche zwei europäischen Länder sind die besten, wenn er im Ausland studieren möchte?

In any order:
- *Schottland* [1]
- *Italien* [1]

The second part of **Question 9** is seemingly straightforward. However, pay attention to the specifics, as there are some tricks!

… Er glaubt, um mein Englisch zu verbessern, sollte ich in den Vereinigten Staaten studieren, oder vielleicht in **Schottland**. *Dort wäre es jedenfalls viel billiger als in England, zum Beispiel. Er hat auch* **Italien** *empfohlen…*

Peter actually mentions **four** countries in this short section - the question requires only two. A closer inspection, however, reveals the correct answers: **Scotland** is recommended <u>instead of</u> England, because it is cheaper; **Italy** is also recommended; and the USA, whilst being cited as a place to improve one's English, isn't a European country!

Mark Scheme 9(b):

0-2	- Award one mark for each correct answer, up to two. - Answers may be in any order. - Deduct a mark for each incorrect answer, even if correct answers are also given. Zero marks is the minimum mark for this question.

Full Transcript:

M: *Ich will in einem anderen europäischen Land studieren. Das Wetter ist dort viel besser als in der Heimat.*

F: *Peter, das ist kein wichtiger Grund. Die deutschen Universitäten sind heutzutage weltweit* **respektiert**.

M: *Stimmt, aber man muss in Deutschland Studiengebühren bezahlen. In vielen europäischen Ländern ist* **ein kostenloses Studium** *noch möglich. Und außerdem sind, nachdem man graduiert hat,* **die Chancen auf dem globalen Arbeitsmarkt viel besser.**

F: *Du hast Recht, und vor allem kann man* **viele neue Freunde kennenlernen und Kontakte knüpfen, das heißt mögliche Geschäftspartner!** *Ich denke aber, ich hätte* **zu viel Heimweh** *und ich könnte mich nicht an die* **kulturellen Unterschiede** *gewöhnen. Jedoch ist es allein deine Entscheidung. Für jeden das Passende.*

M: *Ja, das hat mein Englischlehrer auch gesagt. Er glaubt, um mein Englisch zu verbessern, sollte ich in den Vereinigten Staaten studieren, oder vielleicht in* **Schottland**. *Dort wäre es jedenfalls viel billiger als in England, zum Beispiel. Er hat auch* **Italien** *empfohlen, aber ich müsste erst die Sprache lernen! Klingt gut, oder?*

END OF SOLUTIONS FOR PAPER 2

Listening Paper 3

Visit **rsleducational.co.uk/germanaudio** *to download the audio file for this paper.*

You may pause the recording between questions to allow yourself reading and writing time.

If you wish to complete this paper in timed conditions, allow a maximum of 45 minutes plus 5 minutes of reading time.

Instructions

- Use **black** ink or ballpoint pen.
- Answer **all** questions.
- Answer the questions in the spaces provided.
  - *There may be more space than you require.*
- Dictionaries are not allowed.

Advice

- You have 5 minutes to read through the paper before the recording starts.
- You will hear each extract twice. You may write at any time during the examination. There will be a pause after each question.
- Read each question **carefully** before attempting it.
- The marks available for each question are given in [square brackets]. These give you an indication of how long to spend on each question.
- There is a total of **50 marks** available for this paper.
- Leave time to check your answers at the end, if possible.

Kleidung

1   Was tragen diese Leute? Tragen Sie den richtigen Buchstaben in die Kästchen ein.
     What are these people wearing? Enter the correct letters in the boxes.

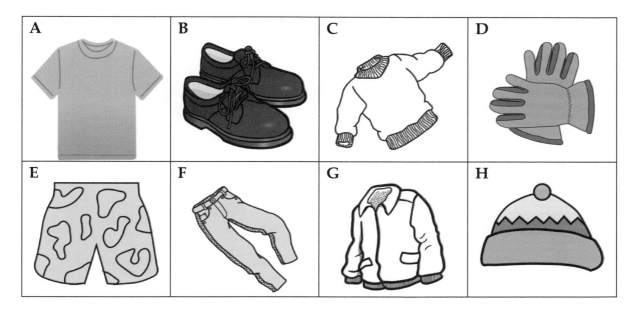

Beispiel: A
(a)
(b)
(c)
(d)

(Total for Question 1 = 4 marks)

Mein Lieblingsfach

2 Was ist das Lieblingsfach jedes Kindes? Tragen Sie den richtigen Buchstaben in die Kästchen ein.

What is each child's favourite subject? Enter the correct letters in the boxes.

A Physics
B German literature
C Physical Education
D French
E Woodwork
F Chemistry
G Maths
H History

(a)
(b)
(c)
(d)

(Total for Question 2 = 4 marks)

Technologie

3   Was sagt Heidi über Technologie? Wählen Sie den richtigen Buchstaben.
What does Heidi say about technology? Choose the correct letter.

A Zeit	**E** Lassen	**I** Verloren
B Langweilig	**F** Freunde	**J** Verbieten
C Vorsichtig	**G** Sympathisch	**K** Verkauft
D Lebensnotwendig	**H** Gefahr	

(a) Für mich ist das Internet ....

(b) Ich habe jetzt mehr ....

(c) Meine Eltern .... mich, spät auszugehen.

(d) Ich habe mein Handy oft ....

(e) Man muss noch .... sein.

(Total for Question 3 = 5 marks)

Nachrichten

4   Hören Sie sich diese Nachrichten an und machen Sie ein Kreuz [X] dort, **wo** die Ereignisse stattgefunden haben.
Jedes Land darf mehr als einmal benutzt werden und die Berichte sind in keiner bestimmten Reihenfolge.

Listen to these news reports and write a cross [X] to show **where** the events took place.
Each country may be used more than once and the reports are in no particular order.

	Beispiel: Wetter	Verkehr	Raub	Sport	Konzert
Deutschland					
Österreich					
Die Schweiz	X				

(Total for Question 4 = 4 marks)

Hotelreservierung

5 Hören Sie sich dieses Gespräch an und beantworten die folgenden Fragen. Kreuzen Sie **[X]** jede richtige Antwort an.

Listen to this conversation and answer the following questions. Put a cross **[X]** in each correct box.

(a) The caller requires…

(i) A single room	
(ii) A double room	
(iii) A room with a view	
(iv) An ensuite room	

(b) The room is…

(i) On the ground floor	
(ii) On the first floor	
(iii) On the second floor	
(iv) On the top floor	

(c) Why are they going to Vienna?

(i) National holiday	
(ii) Work	
(iii) Celebration	
(iv) Visiting family	

(d) What attraction does the receptionist recommend?

(i) Art gallery	
(ii) Palace	
(iii) Zoo	
(iv) Market	
(v) Cathedral	

(e) What time does breakfast start?

(i) 7am	
(ii) 7:30am	
(iii) 8:30am	
(iv) 9am	
(v) 10am	

(f) How much is the room per night?

(i) €70	
(ii) €78	
(iii) €80	
(iv) €87	

(Total for Question 5 = 6 marks)

Wanderfest

6 Hören Sie sich den folgenden Bericht an und markieren mit einem Kreuz [X], welche **fünf** Sätze **richtig** sind.

Listen to the following report and indicate with a cross [X] which **five** sentences are **true**.

A Es ist das größte Fest seiner Art in Europa.	
B Jugendliche sind erlaubt.	
C Das Fest ist am Sonnabend.	
D Mehr als 40.000 Menschen nehmen teil.	
E Es wird musikalische Unterhaltung geben.	
F Einige Touren dauern drei Stunden.	
G Sie wollen sowohl den Tourismus als auch einen gesunden Lebensstil fördern.	
H Es gibt auch andere sportliche Aktivitäten.	
I Der Eintritt kostet €6.000.	
J Man zahlt weniger, wenn man seine Kinder mitbringt.	

(Total for Question 6 = 5 marks)

Rügen

7   Was sagt dieser Bericht über Reiseziele? Schreiben Sie **auf Englisch** die Antworten auf die Fragen.

What does this report say about holiday destinations? Answer the questions **in English**.

(a) Where **exactly** are the most popular destinations for German holidaymakers, according to the report? Give **two** ideas.   [2]

....

....

(b) What can young people do in Rügen? Give **two** ideas.   [2]

....

....

(c) What can adults do?   [1]

....

(d) When exactly do **most** people visit the island?   [1]

....

(e) What is the drawback to visiting Rügen?   [1]

....

(Total for Question 7 = 7 marks)

Internet

8   Diesen Menschen zufolge, was sind die Vor- und Nachteile des Internets?
*Sie sollen **auf Deutsch** und in jedem Kästchen antworten, aber sie müssen **nicht** in ganzen Sätzen schreiben.*

According to these people, what are the advantages and disadvantages of the internet?
*You should write **in German** and in every box, but you do **not** have to write in full sentences.*

Vorteile

Nachteile
Beispiel: Kompliziert für ältere Generationen

(Total for Question 8 = 7 marks)

Silvester

9 Hören Sie sich diesen Bericht an und wählen das treffendste Wort, um die Sätze fertigzustellen.

Listen to this report and choose the most appropriate word to complete each sentence.

Beispiel: "Silvester" ist ein anderer Name für **NEUJAHRSABEND/~~WEIHNACHTEN~~**.

(a) Die Deutschen nennen diesen Tag "Silvester" aufgrund des ehemaligen **PAPSTES/PRÄSIDENTEN**. [1]

(b) Feuerwerke sind **VERBOTEN/POPULÄR**. [1]

(c) Es ist nötig, so viel **LÄRM/WERK/CHAOS** wie möglich machen. [1]

(d) Es ist nicht **ERLAUBT/GENUG/WICHTIG**, zu arbeiten. [1]

(e) Auf Partys wird viel **GESPIELT/GETANZT/GEKÜSST**. [1]

(f) Man versucht, die **ZUKUNFT/FUßBALLERGEBNISSE/MUSIK** vorauszusagen. [1]

(g) Die Leute, die zuhause bleiben, **ESSEN/RADIO HÖREN/SPIELEN/FERNSEHEN/SCHLAFEN/ GEHEN AUS**. (**Two** answers) [2]

(Total for Question 9 = 8 marks)

TOTAL FOR PAPER 3 = 50 MARKS

Blank Page

Listening Paper 3 - SOLUTIONS

Kleidung

1 Was tragen diese Leute?	
(a) *H*	[1]
(b) *D*	[1]
(c) *G*	[1]
(d) *E*	[1]

This question tests simple core GCSE vocabulary on clothes, with four marks available. There are some items mentioned that don't have a corresponding picture.

TOP TIP: Dedicate time to learning vocab.

All the vocabulary tested here is in your GCSE syllabus. Make sure that you know it: the first half of each Listening and Reading Paper is almost entirely focused on vocabulary!

Try to **spend at least ten minutes a day learning vocab**: it will really help with the exam. There are plenty of free apps out there to make it fun. Make it part of your daily routine – as normal as brushing your teeth. When ten minutes a day becomes easy, try fifteen!

The example question is very easy: the word *T-shirt* is the same in English and German! The next speaker says that it is very cold (which is a clue to the kind of clothing item it may be) and that he is wearing a hat and scarf. There is no option for scarf, so **H** is the only possible answer.

The third speaker tells us that he has bought new *Handschuhe*, so the answer is **D** - the literal translation is "hand shoes", but don't write **B** by mistake! The answer to the next question is **G** because the speaker declares that one has to wear a *Regenjacke* (literally "rain-jacket") and an umbrella. The final speaker explains that he prefers wearing *kurze Hosen* because they are fashionable, so the answer is **E** (shorts) and not F (trousers)!

Full Transcript:

M: *Heute trage ich ein T-Shirt.*
F: *Es ist sehr kalt, also trage ich einen **Hut** und einen Schal.*
M: *Ich habe neue **Handschuhe** gekauft.*
F: *Man muss heute eine **Regenjacke** und einen Regenschirm tragen.*
M: *Ich trage lieber **kurze Hosen**, weil sie sehr modisch sind.*

Mark Scheme:

0-4	- Award one mark for each correct answer, up to four. - Incorrect answers do not score. Multiple answers score 0 marks for that question.

Mein Lieblingsfach

2 Was ist das Lieblingsfach jedes Kindes?	
(a) *F*	[1]
(b) *B*	[1]
(c) *D*	[1]
(d) *C*	[1]

There are a few traps in this question, so listen carefully and then select the correct answer after weighing up the options. Make sure you have answered each question, and that you don't have multiple answers for any of them.

The first answer is fairly simple: she says that she loves chemistry (option **F**) because the experiments are interesting, giving you both the key word (*Chemie*) and a very big clue!

The next speaker says that he likes writing stories as well as studying famous works by German writers. The first bit of the sentence doesn't really provide us with an answer, as creative writing isn't given as an option, although you need to understand from context that *Geschichte* refers to writing stories and <u>not</u> history. If there's any remaining doubt, the mention of German writers should give you the correct answer of **B German Literature**: you can only choose one subject per speaker.

The third speaker reveals that she is interested in languages in different countries. The only foreign language listed as an option is **D French**. Remember that German isn't a foreign language for her, as well as the fact that **B** was already used as the answer for the previous speaker! Finally, the fourth speaker tells us that he hates a lot of his school subjects, especially Maths. Therefore, be careful that you don't just hear the word *Mathe* and rush to answer **G**, as this is incorrect. He goes on to say that he prefers being active, so the only possible correct answer is **C Physical Education**.

Full Transcript:

*F: Ich liebe **Chemie**. Die Experimente sind so interessant.*
*M: Ich mag es, Geschichten zu schreiben und ich studiere auch gern berühmte **Werke von deutschen Schriftstellern**.*
*F: Ich interessiere mich für die **Sprachen** in verschiedenen Ländern der Welt.*
*M: Ich hasse viele meiner Schulfächer, besonders Mathe. Ich mag es lieber, **aktiv** zu sein.*

Mark Scheme:

0-4	- Award one mark for each correct answer, up to four. - Incorrect answers do not score. Multiple answers score 0 marks for that question.

Technologie

3 Was sagt Heidi über Technologie?	
(a) *D*	[1]
(b) *F*	[1]
(c) *E*	[1]
(d) *I*	[1]
(e) *C*	[1]

This question requires you to complete a sentence from the choice of words given to you. It is therefore possible (and recommended!) to spend a bit of time before the recording starts and narrow down the choices for each question — See *TOP TIP: Find the possible answers first* in **Listening Paper 2, Question 3**. Is the sentence missing a verb, noun or adjective, for example? Use your grammatical and vocabulary knowledge to eliminate many of the options before even hearing the recording

For example, the answer to **Question 3(a)** is given in the first sentence of the recording:

*Ich weiß nicht, **was ich ohne Internet tun würde.***

You are looking for, most probably, an adjective to complete sentence **3(a)**, which also fits with the sentence "I don't know what I would do without the internet". The only possibly answer is therefore **D Lebensnotwendig** (= essential).

Sentence **3(b)** is most likely missing a noun to follow *mehr*. Either a singular or a plural noun would fit here. The speaker says:

*… habe ich viele neue **Bekannte und Kontakte**, deshalb habe ich auch mehr Verständnis für die Mennschen und deren Probleme.*

In other words, thanks to social media, she has more contacts and acquaintances: **F Freunde**. The following sentence, that she has more understanding for people and their problems, doesn't have a corresponding letter.

Question 3(c) requires a verb that has *mich* as its (direct) object, and must also be third person plural to agree with *meine Eltern*. The two possible options are antonyms of each other: **E Lassen** (= to let, allow, leave) and **J Verbieten** (to forbid). **I Verloren** (= to lose) wouldn't make sense in context. The recording says:

> *Meine Eltern haben oft Angst vor Gefahren, aber heutzutage **ist es mir erlaubt, abends mit meinen Freunden auszugehen**, weil ich mit meinem Handy sicherer bin.*

Although the word *Gefahren* is mentioned, and is one of the options, she actually goes on to say that she is allowed (*es ist mir erlaubt*) to go out with her friends. Therefore the answer is **E Lassen**.

The missing word for **3(d)** is a past participle of a verb, which you know because it follows *haben* and occurs at the end of the clause or sentence. The possible options are **K Gelesen** and **I Verloren**, which were also options for the previous sentence. Verbs with a prefix such as *ver-* don't take *ge-* in the past participle, so usually look the same as their infinitive forms. However, the past participle of **J Verbieten** (to forbid) is *verboten*. **H Gefahr** is a noun, not a past participle (*gefahren* would be the past participle of *fahren*). The answer is revealed when the speaker says:

> *Das Problem ist, ich kann mich selten daran erinnern, **wo ich es gelassen habe**!*

That is, she can rarely remember (*selten* is an antonym of *oft*) where she has left her phone, so the answer is **I Verloren**.

Finally, we require an adjective (one has to be …) to complete sentence **3(e)**. Out of the remaining options, only a handful make sense, and only one corresponds exactly to the recording:

> *Deshalb müssen meine Freunde und ich immer **aufpassen**.*

Aufpassen is a common verb meaning to watch out, or to take care, so the missing word is **C Vorsichtig** (= careful).

Full Transcript:

*F: Ich weiß nicht, **was ich ohne Internet tun würde**. Aufgrund meiner sozialen Medien, beispielsweise Facebook, Instagram usw. [und so weiter], habe ich viele neue **Bekannte und Kontakte**, deshalb habe ich auch mehr Verständnis für die Menschen und deren Probleme.*

*Meine Eltern haben oft Angst vor Gefahren, aber heutzutage **ist es mir erlaubt, abends mit meinen Freunden auszugehen**, weil ich mit meinem Handy sicherer bin. Das heißt ich bin erreichbarer als je zuvor. Das Problem ist, ich kann mich selten daran erinnern, **wo ich es gelassen habe**! Ich weiß auch, dass diese technologischen Fortschritte gefährlich sein können. Es gibt viele Leute, die nicht sehr freundlich sind. Deshalb müssen meine Freunde und ich immer **aufpassen**.*

Mark Scheme:

0-5	- Award one mark for each correct answer, up to five. - Incorrect answers do not score. Multiple answers score 0 marks for that question.

Nachrichten

4 Wo haben die Ereignisse stattgefunden?	
Deutschland — Raub, Sport	[2]
Österreich — Verkehr	[1]
Die Schweiz — Konzert	[1]

This question is tricky because you are listening out for both the **content** of the news event, in order to realise which category it belongs to, as well as the **place** it occurred. There are some well-known cities mentioned, and you are expected to know which country they are located in.

The reports can be summarised into one of the four categories: *Verkehr* (= traffic), *Raub* (= robbery), *Sport*, or *Konzert*. Therefore, before the recording starts, it would be best to think about the kinds of words that will occur in the reports, and make notes throughout to help you. Use the recording and the repeat to confirm your answers.

The **example** question is a good indicator, because it mentions two types of weather events: *Sturm* and *Überschwemmungen* (storm and flooding), as well as the location: *in der Schweiz.*

Although the next report mentions the football stadium, it is because the motorway towards the stadium has been closed due to an accident, and you are advised to take alternative routes. All of this information points to **A Verkehr** and the report begins by stating that this is *in Österreich.*

The following speaker says that the annual marathon is taking place in Cologne (therefore **C Sport**, *Deutschland*), although the concert hall is mentioned as part of the route. The next speaker (female voice) talks about a German rock band playing a free gig in the Swiss countryside (therefore **D Konzert**, *Die Schweiz*). The fourth speaker mentions jewellery (*Halskette* = necklace) that was stolen from a Munich jeweller's and therefore this is **B Raub**, *Deutschland*. The mention of the police also indicates that it is a crime. Note that *Deutschland* is a correct answer for two reports: **B** and **C**.

Full Transcript:

M: *Ein großer **Sturm** in der Schweiz hat zu **Überschwemmungen** in vielen Städten geführt.*

F: *In Österreich ist **die Autobahn** in Richtung des Fußballstadions wegen eines schweren **Unfalls** gesperrt. Bitte nehmen Sie andere **Routen**.*

M: *Morgen findet der jährliche **Marathonlauf** in Köln statt. Die Route beginnt vor der Konzerthalle und endet im Park.*

F: *Die deutsche **Rockband** wird nächsten Monat einen Auftritt in der schweizerischen Landschaft machen. Das Beste? Der Eintritt ist völlig frei.*

M: *Eine wertvolle Halskette wurde gestern aus einem Münchner Juweliergeschäft **gestohlen**. Die Polizei bittet um Hinweise.*

Mark Scheme:

0-4	- Award one mark for each correct answer, up to four. - Deduct one mark for an incorrect answer. - *Therefore, crossing eight boxes would mean four wrong answers, scoring 0 marks.*

Hotelreservierung

5(a) The caller requires…	
(ii) *A double room*	[1]

5(b) The room is…	
(iii) *On the second floor*	[1]

This question is a series of multiple-choice questions to test your understanding of a conversation between a hotel guest and the receptionist. You may make notes on the paper at any time, but only put a **[X]** in the box when you are sure of your answer. The correct pieces of information for **5(a)** and **5(b)** occur in fairly close proximity to each other:

M: *Ich möchte ein nettes Zimmer für mich und meine Frau reservieren. Es ist egal, was für ein **Doppelzimmer** es ist, solange es nicht im Erdgeschoss ist.*
F: *Natürlich. Wir haben ein tolles Zimmer **auf der zweiten Etage** frei.*
M: *Prima!*

At first, the man says that he would like to reserve a room for him and his wife, and then goes onto to say that he doesn't mind what kind of a *Doppelzimmer* it is. This therefore tells you that he is, in fact, booking a double room **(ii)**. He does, however, say that he doesn't want to be on the ground floor (*Erdgeschoss*), and so the reception says that there is a free room on the second floor **(iii)**. (The guest's reaction shows that he accepts this).

5(c) Why are they going to Vienna?	
(iii) Celebration	[1]

5(d) What attraction does the receptionist recommend?

(i)   Art gallery [1]

The guest goes on to explain:

---

*Wir reisen zum ersten Mal nach Wien. Wir haben arbeitsfreie Zeit wegen des **Geburtstags** meiner Frau. Es ist ein Geschenk von ihrer Mutter.*

Despite the mention of family members and work, he actually says that they have time <u>off</u> work because they are celebrating **(iii)** his wife's birthday and the trip was a gift from her mother.

He then asks the receptionist whether she recommends visiting the Schönbrunn Palace (or castle), and she says that it is always crowded with people and animals. It would be better to visit the museum of modern art **(i)**, which is in the town centre.

---

*Die Paläste sind sehr schön, so viel steht fest. Zu dieser Jahreszeit wird es aber eine große Menge an Leuten und Tieren geben. Meiner Meinung nach wäre es besser, das **Museum für moderne Kunst** zu besuchen. Es ist im Stadtzentrum in der Nähe vom Marktplatz.*

5(e) What time does breakfast start?

(ii)   7:30 am [1]

5(f) How much is the room per night?

(ii) €78 [1]

Finally, he asks when breakfast starts and the receptionist confirms that he is right: it starts at half past seven **(ii)**. She then gives the cost of the room: €78 [*achtundsiebzig*] per night **(ii)**. If you are still confused as to why *halb acht* means half past <u>seven</u>, see **TOP TIPS: *Telling the time in German*** and ***Write out numbers*** in **Listening Paper 1, Question 3**).

Full Transcript:

F: *Guten Tag, wie kann ich Ihnen helfen?*

M: *Ich möchte ein nettes Zimmer für mich und meine Frau reservieren. Es ist egal, was für ein **Doppelzimmer** es ist, solange es nicht im Erdgeschoss ist.*

F: *Natürlich. Wir haben ein tolles Zimmer **auf der zweiten Etage** frei.*

M: *Prima! Wir reisen zum ersten Mal nach Wien. Wir haben arbeitsfreie Zeit wegen des **Geburtstags** meiner Frau. Es ist ein Geschenk von ihrer Mutter. Würden Sie uns empfehlen, das Schloss Schönbrunn zu besuchen?*

F: *Die Paläste sind sehr schön, so viel steht fest. Zu dieser Jahreszeit wird es aber eine große Menge Leute und Tiere geben. Meiner Meinung nach wäre es besser, das **Museum für moderne Kunst** zu besuchen. Es ist im Stadtzentrum in der Nähe vom Marktplatz.*

M: *Danke schön. Und Fruhstück ist **von halb acht** bis zehn Uhr, richtig?*

F: *Ja, stimmt. Ein Zimmer kostet **€78 (achtundsiebzig)** pro Nacht - wie möchten Sie zahlen?*

Mark Scheme:

0-6	- Award one mark for each correct answer, up to six. - Incorrect answers do not score. Multiple answers score 0 marks for that question.

Wanderfest

6 Welche fünf Sätze sind richtig?	
B, E, G, H, J	[5]

This question is a step up in difficulty, but remember that you have five minutes before the recording to look at these questions and make things easier for yourself. It is important that you read the sentences underneath first. Use this time to underline the key words in each sentence. Make notes or simply think of synonyms or other ways the recording could paraphrase them to convey the same meaning – see ***TOP TIP: Make good use of the five minutes before the exam*** starts in **Listening Paper 2**, **Question 6**.

After you have selected your answers, be sure to check that you have exactly <u>five</u> crossed.

Going through the recording step-by-step, we can see where the sentences do and don't correspond with the information given. For example:

A Es ist das größte Fest seiner Art in Europa. - FALSE (no cross needed)
B Jugendliche sind erlaubt. - TRUE

We are told that the festival is the oldest and biggest of its kind in <u>Germany</u> (not in Europe) and that this is the first time that young people can take part:

*Das größte und älteste Wanderfest Deutschlands wird diesen Monat stattfinden. Es wird zum ersten Mal gefördert, dass auch **junge Leute teilnehmen können**. Ein guter Tag für die ganze Familie!*

Europa ≠ Deutschland (≠ means NOT the same as)
Jugendliche = junge Leute
Erlaubt = können teilnehmen.

C Das Fest ist am Sonnabend. - FALSE
D Mehr als 40.000 Menschen nehmen teil. - FALSE

Firstly, the event will take place on Sunday (*Sonntag*). The word *Sonnabend* might confuse you, but it is in fact a word for Saturday, and doesn't mean Sunday evening! Think of it as meaning "Sunday eve", or the day <u>before</u> Sunday (as Christmas Eve means the day before Christmas). Secondly, the recording only says that more than 30,000 hikers are expected, making sentence **D** wrong.

> *Sonntag werden in der Stadt Detmold über 30.000 Wanderer aus ganz Deutschland und Europa erwartet. Es wird den ganzen Tag andauern.*

Sonnabend ≠ Sonntag

E Es wird musikalische Unterhaltung geben. - TRUE
F Einige Touren dauern drei Stunden. - FALSE
G Sie wollen sowohl den Tourismus als auch einen gesunden Lebensstil fördern. - TRUE
H Es gibt auch andere sportliche Aktivitäten. - TRUE

There is no mention of the length of some of the walking tours (**F**) but the beauty of the region and healthy living are both promoted, as well as other sporting activities, specifically climbing and two swimming pools.

> *Den ganzen Tag lang gibt es Vorträge und **Konzerte**, sowie auch mehr als 100 verschiedene Wandertouren. Man kann durch diese Touren die Umgebung entdecken. Die Veranstalter möchten **die Schönheit der Region** demonstrieren. Ein weiteres Ziel des Festes ist es auch, interessant und **gesundheitsorientiert** für junge Leute zu sein. Das heißt, es gibt **noch weitere sportliche Attraktionen**, zum Beispiel Klettern und zwei Freibäder.*

Musikalische Unterhaltung = Konzerte
Tourismus = die Schönheit der Region
gesunder Lebensstil = gesundheitsorientiert
andere sportliche Aktivitäten = noch weitere sportliche Attraktionen

I Der Eintritt kostet €6.000. - FALSE
J Man zahlt weniger, wenn man seine Kinder mitbringt. - TRUE

Finally, the price of entry is six <u>hundred</u> Euros, not six thousand. There are special discounts for students and families: bringing your children with you would mean that you pay less!

> *Ein Programm kostet €600, jedoch mit Sonderrabatten für Studenten und **Familien**.*

Man zahlt weniger = Sonderrabatten
Kinder = Familien

Full Transcript:

F: *Das größte und älteste Wanderfest Deutschlands wird diesen Monat stattfinden. Es wird zum ersten Mal gefördert, dass* **junge Leute teilnehmen können.** *Ein guter Tag für die ganze Familie!* **Sonntag** *werden in der Stadt Detmold über 30.000 Wanderer aus ganz Deutschland und Europa erwartet. Es wird den ganzen Tag andauern.*

Den ganzen Tag lang gibt es Vorträge und **Konzerte,** *sowie auch mehr als 100 verschiedene Wandertouren. Man kann durch diese Touren die Umgebung entdecken. Die Veranstalter möchten* **die Schönheit der Region** *demonstrieren. Ein weiteres Ziel des Festes ist es auch, interessant und* **gesundheitsorientiert** *für junge Leute zu sein. Das heißt, es gibt* **noch weitere sportliche Attraktionen,** *zum Beispiel Klettern und zwei Freibäder. Ein Programm kostet €600, jedoch mit Sonderrabatten für Studenten und* **Familien.**

Mark Scheme:

0-5	- Award one mark for each correct answer, up to five. - Deduct one mark for an incorrect answer. - *Therefore, crossing all ten sentences would mean five wrong answers, scoring 0 marks.*

Rügen

7(a) Where exactly are the most popular destinations for German holidaymakers, according to the report? Give two ideas. Any TWO of: - *Munich*   [1] - *North Germany*   [1] - *(North German) Islands*   [1] - *(North German) coast/beach*   [1] - *Rügen (/eine deutsche Insel in der Ostsee)*   [1]   [Maximum 2]

Remember that you have to answer the questions in this section <u>in English</u> and that these longer passages are designed to help the strongest candidates achieve top grades. They may contain unfamiliar words or terms.

Put shorthand responses in the answer spaces, to prevent you from writing in the wrong section when you return to it. Other notes can go elsewhere on the page.

You have to wait until the final sentence of first section for the relevant information for the first answer:

> *... Unter den beliebtesten Reisezielen sind **München**, die **norddeutschen Inseln** und **der Strand an der norddeutschen Küste**.*

Any of those places, correctly translated, would score you a mark (maximum of two points for this question). **Rügen**, the destination mentioned at the start of the next section, is also acceptable as an answer.

7(b) What can young people do in Rügen? Give two ideas.
- *Water sports* [1]
- *Theme/Holiday park* [1]

7(c) What can adults do?
Walks (along the coast/beach) [1]

The recording then turns its attention specifically to Rügen, and mentions that young people can have fun, despite the lack of big cities nearby:

> *Obwohl es keine großen Städte in der Nähe gibt, können die Jugendlichen trotzdem Spaß haben, indem sie **Wassersportarten machen oder den Freizeitpark besuchen**. Für Erwachsene sind die wunderschönen **Wanderwege** entlang der ganzen Küste eine tolle Idee, um sich zu entspannen.*

You need both activities, translated specifically and correctly into English, to get the maximum marks for **Question 7(b)**. The answer to **7(c)** follows immediately afterwards: that adults can go for walks (along the coast) to relax. Simply writing "relax" isn't sufficient to get the mark for this question, as it isn't strictly an activity.

7(d) When exactly do most people visit the island?
Between June and August. [1]

Make sure to read the question carefully: you are asked for the **exact** time or period that **most** people visit the island. Although April-October is mentioned in the recording, we are immediately afterwards told that peak season (*Hauptsaison*) is between June and August.

> *Gäste besuchen Rügen zwischen April und Oktober. Die Hauptsaison liegt zwischen **Juni und August**.*

7(e) What is the drawback to visiting Rügen?
EITHER:
- *(Frequent) Traffic jams/congestion*
OR:
- *Lack of (reliable) public transport* [1]

Finally, you are asked for a drawback to visiting Rügen, and the relevant information is introduced by the speaker with *große Probleme*. However, either reason given in the recording would score you the full mark for this question:

> *Große Probleme sowohl für Bewohner als auch für Urlauber sind **die häufigen Verkehrsstaus** und der **Mangel an zuverlässigen öffentlichen Verkehrsmittel**.*

The problems are frequent traffic jams and also a lack of reliable public transport. Writing "public transport" by itself would get you the mark here, as it would be clear that you are citing it as a general problem.

Full Transcript:

M: *Für viele Jugendliche sind die Sommerferien normalerweise eine Chance, ins Ausland zu fahren. Heutzutage gibt es aber einen neuen Trend: dieses Jahr haben immer mehr deutsche Urlauber entschieden, in Deutschland zu bleiben. Unter den beliebtesten Reisezielen sind **München**, die **norddeutschen Inseln** und **der Strand an der norddeutschen Küste**.*

***Rügen**, eine deutsche Insel in der Ostsee, ist sehr beliebt. Obwohl es keine großen Städte in der Nähe gibt, können die Jugendlichen trotzdem Spaß haben, indem sie **Wassersportarten machen oder den Freizeitpark besuchen**. Für Erwachsene sind die wunderschönen **Wanderwege** entlang der ganzen Küste eine tolle Idee, um sich zu entspannen.*

*Gäste besuchen Rügen zwischen April und Oktober und die Hauptsaison liegt zwischen **Juni und August**. Jedoch ist auch die ruhige Atmosphäre des Winters eine schöne Abwechslung für Großstadtbewohner. Große Probleme sowohl für Bewohner als auch für Urlauber sind **die häufigen Verkehrsstaus** und der **Mangel an zuverlässigen öffentlichen Verkehrsmittel**.*

Internet

---

8 Diesen Menschen zufolge, was sind die Vor- und Nachteile des Internets?

Vorteile

In any order:

- *Einkaufen* [1]
- *Helfen mit Hausaufgaben* [1]
- *(Um leicht/schnell) mit Freunden (in anderen Ländern) in Kontakt zu bleiben.* [1]
- *Filme und Fernsehsendungen anschauen* [1]
- *Man kann es für alles benutzen* [1]
- *Es kann jungen Leuten (enorm) helfen* [1]

[Maximum 4 positives]

Nachteile

Any THREE of (in any order):

- *Gefährlich/Man kennt die Identität der anderen Internetnutzer nicht.* [1]
- *Tyrannen/Internet-Mobbing* [1]
- *Nicht genug Regulierungen/zu viele unkontrollierte Webseiten* [1]
- *Ungesund (die ganze Zeit am Computer zu sitzen).* [1]

[Maximum 3 negatives]

[Maximum 7 marks in total]

This is another long passage of dialogue, in which you have to pick out and write down both positive and negative aspects of the internet. You have to write **in German** but you don't have to write in full sentences. However, *Freunden* isn't enough to score a mark, as it is very vague; try instead: *mit Freunden in Kontakt zu bleiben*.

Look out for words and phrases that introduce **opinions**, such as *ich finde es…*, or *meiner Meinung nach*, or a **counter-argument**, such as *aber* or *andererseits*. See also *TOP TIP: Look for adjectives* in **Listening Paper 1, Question 8**.

The reasons in the recording don't necessarily occur in an ABAB order – there might be two negatives in the same sentence!

Ensure that the reasons you give are different. For example, *Filme und Fernsehsendungen anschauen* is worth one mark when given as an advantage — not one mark for *Filme* and another for *Fernsehsendungen*!

You can see the correct answers given above, as well as where they occur in the transcript below (given in **bold**). The vocabulary used can be found on the specified GCSE vocabulary list for your exam board, but the difficulty lies in training your brain to specifically identify the information when it occurs, as well as whether it is given in a positive or negative context.

Mark Scheme:

0-7	- Award one mark for each correct answer, up to seven. There should be four advantages and three disadvantages, not including the example. They must be in the correct sections. - Each answer must contain clearly separate information or reasons, not an iteration of the same point in different words. - Answers do not have to be in full sentences, but must convey the correct meaning. - Incorrect or repeated answers do not score.

Full Transcript:

F: *Ich bin Mitglied einer älteren Generation und ich finde es so kompliziert, das Internet zu verstehen. Für meine Kinder ist es ganz anders; sie können es für alles benutzen, beispielsweise* **um einzukaufen***. Eltern sehen es als gefährlich, weil* **man nie ganz genau die Identität anderer Internetnutzer kennt***. Experten meinen aber, dass es jungen Leuten enorm helfen kann, besonders mit den* **Hausaufgaben***. Außerdem ist es auch für sie* **leicht und schnell, um mit Freunden in Kontakt zu bleiben***, sogar wenn sie in anderen Ländern sind. Andererseits gibt es auch im Internet viele* **Tyrannen und Internet-Mobbing***. Es ist ein großes Problem für junge Leute. Es sollte mehr Regulierungen geben, denn es gibt meiner Meinung nach* **zu viele unkontrollierte Webseiten***. Es ist auch sehr* **ungesund***, die ganze Zeit am Computer zu sitzen, aber es ist natürlich sehr praktisch,* **Filme und Fernsehsendungen anzuschauen***, wann man will.*

Silvester

9	
(a) *Papstes*	[1]
(b) *populär*	[1]
(c) *Lärm*	[1]
(d) *erlaubt*	[1]
(e) *gespielt*	[1]
(f) *Zukunft*	[1]
(g) *essen*	[1]
(h) *fernsehen*	[1]

Question 9 asks you to select the correct word to complete the sentence. The recording is long, and at times complicated, so listen attentively. There may be some words and terms you are unfamiliar with, but it will often be possible to work out their meanings from the context. Remember that you can take notes at any time and then answer during a pause in the recording, based on your notes and logic. Look out for synonyms!

e.g. *Krach = Lärm* and *nicht erlaubt = absolut verboten.*

The festival is named after the former <u>Pope</u> Silvester I (**8(a)**). Next, we are told that people in Germany celebrate, just like in other countries, with fireworks (**8(b)**). Therefore, they are popular, definitely not forbidden! *Krach* and *Lärm* are synonyms, so the answer to **8(c)** is that people have to make a lot of noise (*laut* carries the same meaning). However, it is not allowed (*nicht erlaubt* = [*absolut*] *verboten*) to work (**8(d)**), and especially to do the laundry.

At *Silvester* parties, many games are played: therefore, the answer to **8(e)** is *gespielt*. *Es wird* + past participle is a particularly German construction and rare at GCSE-level; here it means something like "there is a lot of playing". Recognising the repeated word *Spiele* in the recording may help, even if you can't quite grasp the exact meaning. Some of these games attempt to see into the future (**8(f)**) – *voraussagen* means "to predict". Finally, **8(g)** requires two activities that people do when they stay at home for New Year's Eve: watching TV and eating.

0-8	- Award one mark for each correct answer, up to eight. There are TWO marks available for **Question 8(g)**. - Answer must be clearly indicated, either by circling or underlining, or by deleting the incorrect options. - Incorrect answers or multiple answers do not score.

Full Transcript:

M: *Silvester - das heißt Neujahrsabend in Deutschland - wird aufgrund des ehemaligen* **Papstes** *Silvester I so genannt. Am 31. Dezember fangen die Feste an: genauso wie in anderen Ländern gibt es* **Feuerwerke**, *alkoholische Getränke und lärmende Partys. Man muss so viel* **Krach** *wie möglich machen, um die bösen Geister und Dämonen zu vertreiben. Außerdem ist es* **absolut verboten**, *zu arbeiten, insbesondere die Wäsche zu machen.*

Partygäste werden natürlich viele **Spiele** *machen, um das neue Jahr zu begrüßen und sie werden auch mit verschiedenen traditionellen Spielen versuchen, in die* **Zukunft** *zu sehen. Die Daheimgebliebenen schauen oft* **Fernsehen** *und sie* **essen** *traditionelle Nachspeisen, hauptsächlich Pfannkuchen. Private Feste mit Böllern und Feuerwerken sind auch häufig.*

END OF SOLUTIONS FOR PAPER 3

Listening Paper 4

Visit **rsleducational.co.uk/germanaudio** *to download the audio file for this paper.*

You may pause the recording between questions to allow yourself reading and writing time.

If you wish to complete this paper in timed conditions, allow a maximum of 45 minutes plus 5 minutes of reading time.

Instructions

- Use **black** ink or ballpoint pen.
- Answer **all** questions.
- Answer the questions in the spaces provided.
  - o *There may be more space than you require.*
- Dictionaries are not allowed.

Advice

- You have 5 minutes to read through the paper before the recording starts.
- You will hear each extract twice. You may write at any time during the examination. There will be a pause after each question.
- Read each question **carefully** before attempting it.
- The marks available for each question are given in [square brackets]. These give you an indication of how long to spend on each question.
- There is a total of **50 marks** available for this paper.
- Leave time to check your answers at the end, if possible.

Answer ALL questions

In der Stadt

1   Was suchen diese Personen? Tragen Sie den richtigen Buchstaben in die Kästchen ein.

What are these people looking for? Enter the correct letters in the boxes.

A Stadium
B Hospital
C Car park
D Library
E Market
F Park
G Town centre
H Post Office

Beispiel: A
(a)
(b)
(c)
(d)

[4]

(e) How do you get to the post office? Answer in **English**.   [1]

………………………………………………………………………………………………

(Total for Question 1 = 5 marks)

Sport

2 Welche Sportarten macht dieses Mädchen gern? Kreuzen Sie [X] jede richtige Antwort an.

Which sports does this girl like doing? Put a cross [X] in each correct box.

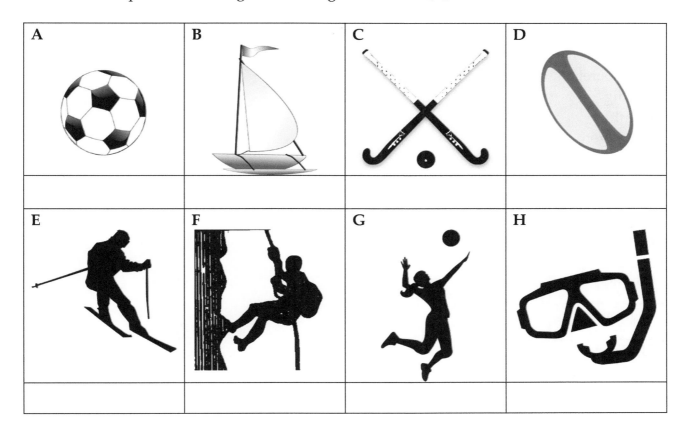

(Total for Question 2 = 4 marks)

Meine Freunde

3 Wie beschreibt Heinrich seine Freunde? Tragen Sie den richtigen Buchstaben in die Kästchen ein. *Jeder Buchstabe darf nur einmal benutzt werden.*

How does Heinrich describe his friends? Enter the correct letters in the boxes. *Each letter may only be used once.*

A Unfreundlich
B Hilfsbereit
C Ruhig
D Faul
E Intelligent
F Gesprächig
G Fleißig
H Fröhlich

(a) Johann	
(b) Theresa	
(c) Monika	
(d) Friedrich	
(e) Thomas	

(Total for Question 3 = 5 marks)

Meine Familie

4   Was sagt Patrizia über ihre Familie? Kreuzen Sie [X] jede richtige Antwort an.
          What does Patrizia say about her family? Put a cross [X] in each correct box.

(a) Wann ist sie geboren?

A 1996	
B 1997	
C 1998	
D 1999	

(b) Wo arbeitet ihre Mutter?

A Hospital	
B School	
C Gym	
D Theatre	

(c) Wie beschreibt sie ihren Vater?

A Clever	
B Fat	
C Boring	
D Friendly	

(d) Wie viele Geschwister hat sie?

A 0	
B 1	
C 2	
D 3	

(e) Wie hilft sie im Haus?

A Washes up	
B Walks the dog	
C Gardening	
D Lays the table	

(Total for Question 4 = 5 marks)

Studien

5   Hören Sie sich diese Studentin an und machen Sie dann ein Kreuz **[X]** in jeder richtigen Kiste, um die entsprechende Zeit zu nennen: die **Vergangenheit**, die **Gegenwart** oder die **Zukunft**.

Listen to this student and then put a cross **[X]** in each correct box to indicate the correct timeframe: the **past**, the **present**, or the **future**.

	Vergangenheit	Gegenwart	Zukunft
(a) Universität			
(b) Wissenschaft			
(c) Mathematik			
(d) Klinikum			

(Total for Question 5 = 4 marks)

Interview

6   Hören Sie sich dieses Interview mit einem Athleten an und schreiben darunter **auf Englisch** die Antworten auf die Fragen. *Sie müssen nicht in ganzen Sätzen schreiben.*

Listen to this interview with an athlete and write your answers to the questions below **in English**. *You don't have to write in full sentences.*

(a) Why did Lothar Matthäus inspire him as a child?   [1]

....

(b) Which precise event does he compete in?   [1]

....

(c) What does he prefer **not** to eat, in order to stay healthy?   [1]

....

(d) How often does he recommend training?   [1]

....

(e) What is his goal for **next** year?   [1]

....

(Total for Question 6 = 5 marks)

Vom Aussterben bedrohte Tiere

7 Hören Sie sich diesen Bericht an und schreiben dann, ob die Information der einzelnen Satzteile **richtig, falsch,** oder **nicht bekannt** ist.

Listen to this report and then write whether the information in each phrase is **correct, false** or **unknown.**

R = Richtig
F = Falsch
NB = Nicht bekannt

(a) Es gibt mehr gefährdete Tiere als je zuvor.	
(b) Es gibt mehr als einen Grund für das Aussterben dieser Tiere.	
(c) Man unternimmt nichts, um bedrohte Tiere zu retten.	
(d) Viele Meeresschildkröten wohnen in der Nähe von Afrika.	
(e) Die Belastung der Weltmeere ist ein großes Problem für Wildtiere.	
(f) Solange es einige Tiere jeder Spezies gibt, wird sie ohne Probleme überleben.	
(g) Jeder Handel mit Wildtieren ist verboten.	
(h) Nashörner können mehr als eine Milliarde Dollar wert sein.	

(Total for Question 7 = 8 marks)

Online-Dating

8   Diesem Bericht zufolge, was sind die Vor- und Nachteile des Online-Datings?
     *Sie sollten **auf Deutsch** und in jedem Kästchen antworten, aber sie müssen **nicht** in ganzen
     Sätzen schreiben.*

     According to this report, what are the advantages and disadvantages of online
     dating?
     *You should answer **in German** and in every box, but you do **not** have to write in full
     sentences.*

Vorteile
Beispiel: Viele Leute in demselben Ort.

Nachteile

(Total for Question 8 = 6 marks)

Die Rehabilitationsklinik

9   Hören Sie sich diesen Bericht an und korrigieren die Sätze, indem Sie ein oder zwei Wörter durchstreichen und ersetzen.

Listen to this report and correct the sentences by crossing out and replacing one or two words.

(a) Die Rehabilitationsklinik ist in der Nähe von München.

....   [1]

(b) Viele der Patienten sind Pensionäre.

....   [1]

(c) Es ist bei der Klinik schwer, die Aufmerksamkeit zu vermeiden.

....   [1]

(d) Die Patientin müssen auch in der Klinik wohnen.

....   [1]

(e) Frau Löw ist Köchin.

....   [1]

(f) Sie sagt, das Wichtigste für die Patienten sei Medizin.

....   [1]

(g) Die Kritiker denken, dass die Klinik viele Forschungen versteht.

....   [1]

(h) Wenn ein Familienmitglied alkoholsüchtig ist, sollte man erst Ärzte suchen.

....   [1]

(Total for Question 9 = 8 marks)
TOTAL FOR PAPER 4 = 50 MARKS

Listening Paper 4 - SOLUTIONS

In der Stadt

1 Was suchen diese Personen?	
(a) *D*	[1]
(b) *F*	[1]
(c) *G*	[1]
(d) *B*	[1]

The correct answers are signalled in **bold** in the transcript given below.

1(e) How do you get to the post office?	
Go left/Turn left	
OR:	
Around the corner	[1]

The second half of **Question 1** requires you to translate the simple set of directions you hear in the recording.

Full Transcript:

M: *Ich suche das Stadion.*

F: *Wo ist die **Bibliothek**?*

M: *Gibt es in der Nähe einen **Park**?*

F: *Entschuldigen Sie bitte, wie komme ich zum **Stadtzentrum**?*

M: *Ich brauche sofort ein **Krankenhaus** - es ist ein Notfall!*

F: *Entschuldigung, wie kommt man zur Post?*

M: *Gehen Sie hier **links um die Ecke**.*

Mark Scheme:

0-4	- Award one mark for each correct answer, up to five. - Incorrect answers do not score. Multiple answers for (a) to (d) score 0 marks for that question.

Sport

2 Welche Sportarten macht dieses Mädchen gern?	
B, C, F, G	[4]

This exercise requires you to identify the four sports that the speaker **enjoys** doing - not just the ones that she mentions. You need to cross **exactly** four boxes!

Remember to listen out for clues and vocabulary, and don't stop listening once you think you have heard the right word – there may be traps! See *TOP TIP: Pay attention to the whole sentence* in **Listening Paper 1, Question 2**.

She explicitly says that she particularly enjoys hockey (**C**) as it is faster and more tactical than football. By implication, therefore, she doesn't enjoy football as much. She then says that rugby is too violent (*zu gewalttätig*) for her. Even if you didn't know the word *gewalttätig*, the word *zu* implies a negative opinion: too much of anything is a bad thing! She therefore prefers volleyball (**G**), especially beach volleyball.

She is not really bothered about water sports (*Wassersportarten sind mir egal*), apart from sailing (**B**), which she says she loves. She also uses the word *gern* to say that her <u>Dad</u> likes skiing, but she has never done it. She says that it's a lot more fun – and just as active – to go climbing (**F**) outdoors.

Full Transcript:

F: *Ich spiele gerne viele Sportarten, besonders* **Hockey**. *Es ist viel schneller und taktischer als Fußball. Rugby ist zu gewalttätig für mich, also spiele ich lieber* **Volleyball**, *am liebsten am Strand. Wassersportarten sind mir egal, außer* **Segeln**. *Ich liebe das! Mein Vati fährt gern Ski, aber das habe ich nie getan. Ich habe viel mehr Spaß beim* **Klettern** *im Freien. Es ist genauso aktiv.*

Mark Scheme:

0-4	- Award one mark for each correct answer, up to four. - Deduct one mark for each incorrect answer, even if the correct answers are also crossed. - *Therefore, crossing all eight boxes would mean four wrong answers and score 0 marks.*

Meine Freunde

3 Wie beschreibt Heinrich seine Freunde?	
(a) *Johann:* B	[1]
(b) *Theresa:* E	[1]
(c) *Monika:* G	[1]
(d) *Friedrich:* C	[1]
(e) *Thomas:* H	[1]

Choose the option that fits **best**.

Read the options before the recording starts, so you know the sort of information you are listening for and are able to identify it when you hear it. The recording is highly unlikely to use exactly the same adjectives as the ones provided, so think of synonyms and ways of paraphrasing them.

The first person Heinrich tells us about is Johann, who he says always supports him when it is necessary and that no problem is too big for him. Therefore the option that fits best here is **B Hilfsbereit** (= "helpful").

Then we have two similar answers. Theresa normally gets the best grades (*Noten* = "grades", not "notes!") — so the answer <u>seems to be</u> a choice between **E Intelligent** or **G Fleißig** — while Monika works a lot, giving **G Fleißig**. However, we are told that "each letter may only be used once", so Theresa can <u>only</u> be **E Intelligent**.

Friedrich, on the other hand, is **not** talkative (*plaudern* = "to chat"): he is **C Ruhig**, whereas Thomas is always laughing and in a good mood, therefore **H Fröhlich**.

Full Transcript:

M: *Hallo, ich heiße Heinrich. Mein bester Freund heißt Johann und **er unterstützt mich immer**, wenn es nötig ist. Kein Problem ist zu groß für ihn.*
*Theresa erreicht normalerweise **die besten Noten**, aber sie erlaubt uns nicht, ihre Arbeit zu kopieren. Monika ist auch eine Lieblingsstudentin unseres Lehrers, weil **sie so viel arbeitet**.*
*Ich mag auch Friedrich. **Er plaudert nicht viel**, aber wir sind gut befreundet.*
*Thomas ist ein sehr netter Mensch, der **ständig lächelt**. Er ist **immer in sehr guter Stimmung** und ich finde das fantastisch.*

Mark Scheme:

0-5	- Award one mark for each correct answer, up to five. - Incorrect answers do not score. Multiple answers score 0 marks for that question.

Meine Familie

4(a) Wann ist sie geboren?	
C - 1998	[1]

Question 4(a) simply requires careful listening - there are no tricks here, but numbers, times, and dates are often initially difficult to comprehend for non-native speakers. The answer is 1998: *ein Tausend neunhundertachtundneunzig.* Remember that for German double-digits you say "eight and ninety" for ninety-eight - see *TOP TIP: Write out numbers* in **Listening Paper 1, Question 3.**

4(b) Wo arbeitet ihre Mutter?
B - School   [1]

The next question requires a **place** connected with a profession, and Patrizia says:

---

*Meine Mutti ist **Direktorin eines Gymnasiums** am Stadtrand und mein Vati ist Arzt.*

Only one of the options can be right, and it is **B School**, because she is a headteacher. You may have heard *Direktorin* and thought of a theatre director, but this is a false friend. Remember also that *Gymnasium* is a type of school (similar to a grammar school) and not a gym (*Fitnesszentrum*). Her father is a doctor, so **he** is the one who would work in a hospital.

4(c) Wie beschreibt sie ihren Vater?
D - Friendly   [1]

Next, you are asked to choose the most apt adjective to describe her father, based on what she says. **Friendly** matches *sympathisch*, so **D** is the correct answer. A common confusion for English speakers is that *groß* means tall, not fat.

4(d) Wie viele Geschwister hat sie?
A - 0   [1]

She then goes onto say that she is an only child (*Einzelkind*) - even though her two best friends are **like** sisters to her, and she **would like** to have an elder brother - so the answer is that she has **no** siblings (**A**).

4(e) Wie hilft sie im Haus?
B - Walk the dog   [1]

She helps at home (due to the lack of brothers and sisters) and walks the dog every morning before breakfast (**B**), so that it doesn't go in the garden - nothing to do with gardening!

Full Transcript:

F: *Ich bin **1998** in Hannover geboren. Meine Mutti ist **Direktorin eines Gymnasiums** am Stadtrand und mein Vati ist Arzt. Er ist ein großer Mensch und immer sehr **sympathisch**. Wir kommen sehr gut miteinander aus. Ich bin **Einzelkind,** aber meine zwei besten Freundinnen sind für mich wie Schwestern. Ich hätte auch gern einen älteren Bruder, der mir helfen könnte, aber leider habe ich keinen. Deshalb muss ich im Haus helfen. Das heißt, ich muss allmorgendlich vor dem Frühstück **mit dem Hund Spazieren gehen**, so dass er nicht auf die Toilette in unserem Garten geht!*

Mark Scheme:

0-5	- Award one mark for each correct answer, up to five. - Incorrect answers do not score. Multiple answers score 0 marks for that question.

Studien

5 Zeigen Sie die entsprechende Zeit:	
(a) Universität — *Gegenwart*	[1]
(b) Wissenschaft — *Zukunft*	[1]
(c) Mathematik — *Gegenwart*	[1]
(d) Klinikum — *Vergangenheit*	[1]

This question asks you identify the appropriate timeframe (past, present, or future) for four aspects of a student's life.

In many cases, the tenses in the recording will give you the biggest clue as to the timeframe in question, but other answers may require a bit more attention. Look out for phrases such as *letzten Monat/letztes Jahr* (past), *nächsten Monat/nächstes Jahr* (future), *vor zwei Jahren* (two years **ago**, i.e. past) and *wenn ich älter bin* (when I am older, i.e. future).

She begins by saying that she is a student at the University of Bonn (therefore **5(a)** is in the present tense). Although we don't know what it is she is currently studying, she says that she **would like to** study (*würden* + infinitive) physics, even though she has never done it at school. The conditional tense tells us that the answer to **5(b)** is *Zukunft*. The second half of the sentence, that she has never studied it in school (present perfect tense) isn't actually relevant. This is confirmed when she says that she will change course next September (both *Nächsten September* and *werden* + infinitive tells us that this is a **future** event).

Therefore, she has to undergo a Maths preparation course, in order to be ready for next year. In other words, even though she says that she **started** the course last week (*ich habe letzte Woche ... angefangen*), the answer to **5(c)** is *Gegenwart* because the course is ongoing (*wöchentliche* = weekly): she will finish next year.

The answer to **5(d)** is the Past (*Vergangenheit*). Instead of the word *Klinikum* in the question, the recording mentions the more commonplace *Krankenhaus*. We can tell that this information is a past event from the Imperfect Tense (*musste ich*) and because it happened when she was six years old (*mit sechs Jahren*). She also says that she hopes never to return in the future, but this is a red herring and a distraction from the correct answer.

Full Transcript:

*F: Ich bin Studentin an der Universität Bonn. Ich mag meinen Kurs, aber ich würde lieber **Physik** studieren, obwohl ich es nie in der Schule gehabt habe. Nächsten September werde ich den Kurs ändern. Ich habe letzte Woche einen wöchentlichen **Mathe-Vorbereitungskurs** angefangen, um nächstes Jahr fertig zu sein, aber nur wenn ich gesund bleiben kann. Mit sechs Jahren musste ich mit einer Lungeninfektion ins **Krankenhaus** und ich hoffe, nie in der Zukunft zurückgehen zu müssen.*

Mark Scheme:

0-4	- Award one mark for each correct answer, up to four. - Incorrect answers do not score. Multiple answers score 0 marks for that question.

Interview

6 (a) Why did Lothar Matthäus inspire him as a child? EITHER: *- He was hard-working/determined* OR: *- He (always) gave everything he had* OR: *- (His) passion/zeal*	[1]

For longer passages with complex language, remember that you may find it useful to refer to my *TOP TIP: Make shorthand notes* in **Listening Paper 1, Question 7(a)**. Also, don't forget to answer in English (the questions are also in English!) and to make sure that your answers are precise and accurately reflect the recording. Don't copy **too much** information directly, as it's a waste of time and may show that you haven't understood the text well enough to be able to use your own words.

There may be words and terms you are unfamiliar with, but it will often be possible to work out their meanings from the context. Any notes you make can be used to help you quickly remember the question.

Lothar Matthäus (it doesn't matter if you don't know who he is!) is mentioned immediately by the speaker, who gives several reasons why he is his favourite sportsman:

*Als Kind war mein Lieblingssportler Lothar Matthäus, weil er immer **so fleißig war**. Er hat immer alles gegeben, was er hatte. Er war inspirierend. Heute versuche ich immer, dieselbe Leidenschaft zu haben, wann auch immer ich renne.*

The correct translation of any of these reasons is enough to score the mark for this question (see the model answer given above). There is no need to give more than one reason, so choose the one you are most confident about. Note that simply saying "he was inspiring" is not an answer to the question "Why did Lothar Matthäus inspire him"!

6(b) Which precise event does he compete in?
- *1500 metres* [1]

The next question asks for the event that the interviewee currently competes in (NB present tense!), therefore we can discount the first half of his sentence, because it is in the wrong tense:

---

*Ich bin als Kind 400-Meter-Hürdenlauf gerannt, aber jetzt renne ich nur noch **1500-Meter-Lauf**.*

Remember to revise numbers in German and practise identifying them when you hear them - *TOP TIP: Write out numbers* in **Listening Paper 1, Question 3.**

6(c) What does he prefer not to eat, in order to stay healthy?
- *Red meat* [1]

This question is slightly trickier, although the key word is highlighted in **bold** in the question: what does he prefer **not** to eat? Some questions are very specific in the information they require - see *TOP TIP: Always read the question carefully* in **Listening Paper 1, Question 6.**

The speaker lists a couple of foodstuffs that **are** key to a healthy diet, as well as the supposed idea that one should avoid fatty food. However, he says that this is not true! He does however try to avoid red meat. The key word is *vermeiden* (= "to avoid") so don't get distracted by the extraneous information in the recording. Your translation also has to be accurate here: simply writing that he avoids meat would not gain you a mark, as it is not true; you have to be specific and say <u>red</u> meat!

---

*Es ist lebensnotwendig, gesundes Essen zu essen: Kohlenhydrate, Eiweiß usw. Man sagt, dass man keine fetthaltigen Lebensmittel essen sollte, aber das ist nicht wahr. Ich versuche jedoch, **rotes Fleisch** zu vermeiden.*

(d) How often does he recommend training?
- *Every other day/Once every two days* [1]

Next, the speaker reveals his training regime. Note again the specifics of the question when answering it:

> *Die Mehrheit meiner Kollegen trainiert die ganze Zeit, das heißt von 9 Uhr bis 18 Uhr jeden Tag. Völliger Unsinn! Viel besser wäre es, das **jeden zweiten Tag** zu machen, so dass du dich erholen kannst.*

That is, the majority of his colleagues train nine hours a day every day. He says that this is *völliger Unsinn* — a fantastic expression meaning "complete rubbish", in case you want to steal this for use in the speaking exam! Instead, he says that it is much better (remember, the question asks what he <u>recommends</u>) to train every other day, so that you can recover.

(e) What is his goal for next year?
- <u>Compete/Take part</u> in the (Olympic) Games (with Germany)   [1]

The last question is also specific: what is his goal for <u>next year</u>? The final part of the recording mentions his dreams and end-goals:

> *Mein Endziel? Gold in den Olympischen Spielen zu gewinnen, natürlich. Das wird sicher einige Jahre dauern. Zu dieser Zeit im nächsten Jahr hoffe ich, **an den Spielen mit Deutschland teilzunehmen**.*

Although his eventual end-target is to win gold in the Olympics, he recognises that this will take a few years. However, this time next year he hopes to be at least participating in the (Olympic) Games with Germany — *teilnehmen* is literally "to take part".

Full Transcript:

M: *Als Kind war mein Lieblingssportler Lothar Matthäus, weil er immer **so fleißig war**. Er hat immer alles gegeben, was er hatte. Er war inspirierend. Heute versuche ich immer, dieselbe Leidenschaft zu haben, wann auch immer ich renne. Ich bin als Kind 400-Meter-Hürdenlauf gerannt, aber jetzt renne ich nur noch **1500-Meter-Lauf**. Es ist lebensnotwendig, gesundes Essen zuzubereiten: Kohlenhydrate, Eiweiß usw. Man sagt, dass man keine fetthaltigen Lebensmittel essen sollte, aber das ist nicht wahr. Ich versuche jedoch, **rotes Fleisch** zu vermeiden.*

*Selbstverständlich trainiere ich viel. Die Mehrheit meiner Kollegen trainiert die ganze Zeit, das heißt von 9 Uhr bis 18 Uhr jeden Tag. Völliger Unsinn! Viel besser wäre es, das **jeden zweiten Tag** zu machen, so dass du dich erholen kannst. Mein Endziel? Gold in den Olympischen Spielen zu gewinnen, natürlich. Das wird sicher einige Jahre dauern. Zu dieser Zeit im nächsten Jahr hoffe ich, **an den Spielen mit Deutschland teilzunehmen**.*

Vom Aussterben bedrohte Tiere

7 Richtig, falsch, oder nicht bekannt?	
(a) *R*	[1]
(b) *R*	[1]
(c) *F*	[1]
(d) *NB*	[1]
(e) *R*	[1]
(f) *F*	[1]
(g) *F*	[1]
(h) *NB*	[1]

This question is about endangered animal species and features some complex language and vocabulary. You are asked to identify whether each statement given corresponds to the information you hear in the recording, or not, or if it is not mentioned. Use your knowledge of synonyms and antonyms.

For example, **sentence (a)** says that there are more endangered animals than ever before (*mehr als je zuvor*), which corresponds to the recording: *immer mehr* (more and more/increasingly more) *Tiere sind heutzutage vom Aussterben bedroht*. **Sentence (b)** states that there is more than one reason for this, and the recording gives at least two reasons: *In vielen Fällen… In anderen [Fällen]…* Therefore, these statements are both true (*richtig*).

The next statement, **sentence (c)**, that nothing is being done to save endangered animals, is false (*falsch*), as the recording states that *Viele Versuche sind in vollem Gange* (many attempts are well underway) to breed endangered species, in order to guarantee their survival. Several species of animals are mentioned, including *Meeresschildkröte* (sea turtles). This word is also given in **sentence (d)**, so should make you listen attentively, even if you don't know the meaning of the word! The suggestion that many turtles are found near Africa isn't mentioned at all, however, so **sentence (d)** is *nicht bekannt*.

The pollution of the sea (*die Belastung der Weltmeere = der Verschmutzung der Meere*) is mentioned as a problem, therefore **sentence (e)** is *richtig*. However, **sentence (f)** is *falsch*, because it suggests that as long as there are some animals of each species, they will survive without any problems. However, the recording says that there **will be** problems: namely, *Krankheiten und Tod* (because their gene pool can't be intermixed well). Don't worry about the specifics of the theory or vocabulary; just focus on the question that is being asked! The sentence *Kein Problem, solange die Menschheit Geld machen kann, oder?* is said sarcastically.

Finally, we are told that **only** trading with protected species is illegal, meaning that **sentence (g)** (*Jeder Handel mit Wildtieren ist verboten*) is *falsch* and the trade of young species of animals is a very profitable industry. In **sentence (h)**, the price of *Nashörner* (rhinos — but again, it doesn't matter if you don't know this word, as long as you recognise it in the recording!) is **not** mentioned (*nicht bekannt*).

Mark Scheme:

0-8	- Award one mark for each correct answer, up to eight. - Incorrect answers do not score. Multiple answers score 0 marks for that question.

Full Transcript:

F: ***Immer mehr Tiere*** *sind heutzutage vom Aussterben bedroht.* ***In vielen Fällen*** *haben sie ihren natürlichen Lebensraum verloren.* ***In anderen*** *ist die Jagd von Menschen Schuld.*

Viele Versuche *sind in vollem Gange, bedrohte Tierarten zu vermehren, um das Überleben der Art zu garantieren, zum Beispiel die Ostafrikanischen Berggorillas, die in Gefangenschaft aufgezogen werden müssen. Außerdem gibt es viele Arten von Meeresschildkröten. Sie sind nicht nur Opfer der Jagd, sondern auch* ***der Verschmutzung der Meere.***

Die Tiergärten und Reservate versuchen, jede Tierart durch Vermehrung zu sichern. Wenn es wenige Tiere gibt, kann das Erbgut nicht gut durchgemischt werden. ***Krankheiten und Tod*** *sind das Ergebnis. Kein Problem, solange die Menschheit Geld machen kann, oder?* ***Nur der Handel von geschützten Tierarten ist illegal***, *besonders bestimmte gefährdete Wildtiere, beispielsweise afrikanische Nashörner. Der Handel mit Jungtieren ist leider eine sehr kostbare Industrie.*

Online-Dating

8 Diesem Bericht zufolge, was sind die Vor- und Nachteile des Online-Datings? **Vorteile** In any order: - *Preisgünstig/Billig OR Kostenfreie Probezeit* [1] - *(Ganz) wirksam/erfolgreich/effektiv.* OR *Jede fünfte (20%) Beziehung beginnt online.* [1] - *(Dating-Apps sind) schnell/praktisch.* [1] [Max. 3 Positives]

Nachteile

Any THREE of these, in any order:

- *Es führt/sie führen zur <u>Abhängigkeit</u>.* [1]

- *Man betrachtet es als <u>ein Spiel mit keinen/ohne wirklichen Folgen.</u>* [1]

- *Man fällt/spricht das Urteil (über jemanden).* [1]

- *(aufgrund von) oberflächlichen Gründen.* OR *Man wird wählerisch/beurteilend/oberflächlich.* [1]

- *Verbrechen* [1]

- *Identitätsbetrug* [1]

- *Man kann viel Geld verlieren.* OR *Falsche Profile* [1]

- *Dein Standort ist sichtbar.* OR *Jemand könnte herausfinden, wo du wohnst etc.* [1]

[Max. 3 Negatives]

[Maximum 6 marks in total]

This is another long passage of dialogue, in which you have to hear and identify positive and negative aspects of the internet. There are several ways of getting full marks for this question.

Look out for adjectives (see also *TOP TIP: Look for adjectives* in **Listening Paper 1, Question 8)**, opinions, and **counter-arguments**. Remember that you don't have to write in full sentences, but you do have to **write in German**. The reasons in the recording don't necessarily occur in an ABAB order.

Make sure that the reasons you give are **different**: for example, the idea that dating websites are effective (*wirksam*) and the statistic which backs this up (*jede fünfte Beziehung hat heutzutage Online begonnen*) are the same point. Often, one word or a simple phrase will suffice to convey the idea, and you don't have to put down the entire phrase from the recording, which is often in complicated German.

You can find the correct answers above, as well as seeing where they occur in the transcript below (given in **bold**). For example, the fact that there are many (single) people in the same place is given as early as the first sentence (this is the **example** given), and the speaker goes on to say that online dating is also fairly cheap (*preisgünstig = billig*), with some websites even offering a free trial period. Either of these things would gain a mark — although not both, as the second point is part of the first idea (that these websites are affordable.)

The next section then offers a slight contradiction: on the one hand, these websites can claim to be effective, given that one fifth of relationships nowadays start online; on the other hand, the speaker asks whether the websites are <u>too</u> effective, and have become **a form of**

addiction. Both arguments are valid, so it would be acceptable to write them both. Make sure that they are in the correct sections!

The (female) speaker goes on to say that some treat the websites like a game with no real consequences, and that there is a danger of becoming too picky, judgemental, or superficial. These are all disadvantages, but only one can get a mark: they all come under an overall idea, that dating websites can have a negative effect on behaviour/personality.

Next we hear a male speaker who begins with *"Auf der anderen Seite"* (on the other hand), therefore introducing a counter-argument – even though we have already heard some negatives. He lists the disadvantages of online dating, including fake profiles and crimes such as identify theft. He also offers the advantages that it is easy and practical (*schnell und praktisch*) to set up a profile, but tempers this with the danger that your location is visible and anyone could find out where you live.

Mark Scheme:

0-6	- Award one mark for each correct answer, up to six: three advantages and three disadvantages, not including the example. They must be in the correct sections. - Each answer must contain clearly separate information or reasons, not reiterations of the same point in different words. - Incorrect or repeated answers do not score.

Full Transcript:

F: *Beim Online-Dating kann man sicher sein, dass es viele ledige Leute in demselben Ort gibt und außerdem ist es ziemlich **preisgünstig**, besonders bei Dating-Seiten, die eine kostenfreie Probezeit anbieten.*

*Diese Webseiten können auch behaupten, sie seien **wirksam**: jede fünfte Beziehung hat heutzutage Online begonnen. Ist es aber <u>zu</u> erfolgreich? Mehrere Untersuchungen zeigen, dass es **eine Art Abhängigkeit** ist, diese Webseiten ständig zu benutzen. Man betrachtet es als ein Spiel mit keinen wirklichen Folgen. Es besteht die Gefahr, dass **man wählerisch wird** und dass man das Urteil über jemanden fällt, aufgrund von oberflächlichen Gründen.*

M: *Auf der anderen Seite gibt es gute Gründe, diese Webseiten zu vermeiden, nämlich Verbrechen. Das heißt, man kann leicht Opfer von **Identitätsbetrug** werden und viele Leute sind um eine Menge Geld von falschen Profilen betrogen geworden. Abgesehen von den Webseiten existieren heute verschiedene Dating-Apps für das Handy. Es ist **schnell und praktisch**, ein Profil zu erstellen, aber natürlich gibt es auch hier noch Gefahren. Anders gesagt: **dein Standort ist sichtbar und jemand könnte herausfinden, wo du wohnst.***

Die Rehabilitationsklinik

> **9**
>
> **(a)** ~~München~~ → *Berlin*
>
> **(b)** ~~Pensionäre~~ → *Promis*
>
> **(c)** ~~schwer~~ → *leicht(er) / einfach(er)*
>
> **(d)** ~~wohnen~~ → *arbeiten*
>
> **(e)** ~~Köchin~~ → *Chefin*
>
> **(f)** ~~Medizin~~ → *Ünterstutzung/Hilfe*
>
> **(g)** ~~versteht~~ → *ignoriert*
>
> **(h)** ~~Ärzte~~ → *Rat*

This final question asks you to listen and respond **in German** by replacing one word to correct the sentences. This recording takes the form of a news report on a rehabilitation clinic with a difference.

There is a lot of information, but you only need specific pieces of information to ascertain which element of the sentence is incorrect. For example, in **9(a)** the incorrect word is *München* as the clinic is in fact near *Berlin*. Clearly mark which word is incorrect and then write the replacement word underneath – you don't need to write out the whole sentence!

9(b) is incorrect because many of the patients are not old-age pensioners, but celebrities (*Promis*). One of the reasons they go to the clinic (**9(c)**) is because it is easier (not hard) to avoid attention (*Aufmerksamkeit* = *Öffentlichkeit*). It is not mentioned whether the patients live in the clinic (**9(d)**), but they do <u>work</u> there (*Die Patienten sind auch die Angestellten* means "The patients are also the employees").

Frau Löwin is the <u>boss</u>, not the cook (**9(e)**) – *Chef* is a false friend and has nothing to do with the English word "chef". She says that the clinic concentrates on mutual support (*Unterstützung*), rather than medicine (drugs) or short-term abstinence (**9(f)**). However, critics of the clinic (**9(g)**) say that it ignores (not "understands" = *verstehen*) decades of research. Finally, **9(h)** is looking for the piece of advice about what people should do **first** (*erst*) if a family member is an alcoholic. The recording says that you should seek **advice** <u>straight away</u> (*sofort*) before seeking a doctor.

Mark Scheme:

0-8	- Award one mark for each correct answer, up to eight. - Answer must include both the deleted word **and** the new word. - Incorrect answers do not score. - Misspelt answers are acceptable if the intended word is clearly understood.

Full Transcript:

M: *Eine Rehabilitationsklinik, die am nördlichen Rand von **Berlin** steht, ist ein beliebtes Ziel für viele **Promis** wegen seiner außergewöhnlichen Methode. Die Patienten sind hier aus mehreren Gründen: um ähnliche Leute kennenzulernen, von den Versuchungen des Stadtzentrums wegzubleiben, oder einfach die Medien und **die Öffentlichkeit zu vermeiden**. Der Unterschied der Methoden dieser Klinik? **Die Patienten sind auch die Angestellten**! Qualifizierte Therapeuten gibt es natürlich, aber die Selbsthilfegruppen, Nachsorge und Workshops liegen in der Verantwortung der Klienten. **Die Chefin** ist Frau Angela Löw:*

F: *Das Problem ist nicht der Alkohol selbst, sondern die Reaktion des Körpers und des Gehirns. Deshalb konzentrieren wir uns auf gemeinsame **Unterstützung**, anstatt Medizin oder Kurzzeitabstinenz. **Die Patienten helfen einander**, weil sie das Erlebnis der anderen wirklich verstehen.*

M: *Es gibt jedoch einen großen Widerstand von der akademischen Gemeinschaft. Einige Lektoren an der Universität Mannheim glauben, die Klinik schaffe ein gefährliches Beispiel, das jahrzehntelange Forschung **ignoriert**.*

*Wenn du jemanden kennst, der vielleicht ein Alkoholproblem hat, musst du **sofort Rat suchen**. Dann können sie einander mit Ehrlichkeit zuhören und miteinander sprechen, bevor man einen Arzt aufsucht.*

END OF SOLUTIONS FOR PAPER 4

Oral (Speaking) Primer

Visit **www.rsleducational.co.uk/germanaudio** to download the conversation recordings discussed in this guide..

The recordings demonstrate how to approach the oral examinations in German and feature a genuine GCSE student. They cover the **conversation** section of the oral (speaking) exam. This is the part that many students fear most, and may not know how to prepare for properly.

This section explains how to improve your grade in this part of the exam, and also provides mark grids.

According to the exam board you are with, other sections of the oral exam may include a role play, a short presentation on a topic of your choosing (with follow-up questions from the examiner), and a discussion of a photo card or picture of your choosing (with follow-up questions based on one of the topics). Some boards use a mixture of these (see below).

Exams involving role-play and/or presentation sections are best prepared for by revising the conversation topics below, making sure you have learnt topic-specific vocabulary and expressions. Remember that the questions will test your ability to **describe** and form **opinions**, your **vocabulary**, and the **past** and **future** tenses. Your teacher will be able to provide further guidance and structure, according to your exam board.

The **example questions** on pages 117-119 are intended to help prepare for the general conversation aspect of the oral exam, but may also be good preparation for other parts of your GCSE preparation.

Mark Scheme:

The following mark schemes **are designed to be useful when preparing for any exam board** and can be used by all students.

There are three mark grids to be applied to the general conversation section: communication and content, interaction and spontaneity, and linguistic knowledge and accuracy. These are worth 12 marks each, giving a total of **36 marks**.

The marking system below reflects the **Edexcel GCSE** criteria, in which each section has an equal weight, giving a total of 36 marks. The exam also includes a role play and a picture-based task.

Edexcel IGCSE gives more weight to the first section – **Communication and Content** – which is also worth 12 marks, but the other sections are worth 8 marks each, making a total of 28 for the Conversation section. A maximum of two topics will be tested in the general conversation. There will also be a discussion of a picture of your choosing, relating to a third topic, which will then lead into a general conversation based on that topic.

AQA GCSE gives an equal weight to each section (10 marks each for total of 30) and includes Pronunciation and Intonation as part of the **Interaction and Spontaneity** mark grid. There is also a role-play and a photo card.

Cambridge IGCSE is also out of 30, but groups the **Communication and Content** and **Interaction and Spontaneity** mark grids together (15 marks), with another 15 marks for **Range and Accuracy of Language**. A further 10 marks are awarded according to Impression, which assesses your overall performance in the Speaking exam, including the role-play, the topic presentation (with further conversation questions on this topic), and the general conversation section.

Communication and Content

0	• No rewardable material.
1-3	• Candidate communicates some relevant information according to the topic and question, occasionally extending their sentences. • Candidate gives straightforward ideas and opinions, occasionally justifying them. • Candidate's vocabulary is limited and straightforward, sometimes resulting in limited communication. • Candidate's pronunciation is often intelligible and clear, with occasional inaccuracies resulting in lost clarity of communication.
4-6	• Candidate communicates relevant information according to the topic and question, with some extended sequences of speech. • Candidate occasionally uses creative language to express opinions and ideas, and occasionally justifies them. • Candidate's vocabulary features some variety, including some uncommon or complex language, resulting in mostly clear communication. • Candidate's pronunciation is intelligible, with minimal inaccuracies that do not result in lost clarity of communication.

7-9	• Candidate communicates relevant information in detail according to the topic and question, usually extending their sentences and sequences of speech. • Candidate frequently uses creative language to express and justify ideas and opinions. • Candidate's vocabulary varies, including frequent uncommon language and a variety of expressions. • Candidate's pronunciation is often intelligible and is predominantly accurate.
10-12	• Candidate communicates detailed and relevant information according to the topic and question, consistently using extended sequences of speech. • Candidate uses creative language to express and justify a wide variety of ideas and opinions throughout. • Candidate uses a wide variety of vocabulary, including frequent uncommon language, and a variety of expressions/structures for different purposes. • Candidate's pronunciation is consistently intelligible and accurate.

In other words, you are required to use language **creatively** to convey your ideas and experiences. Use as much topic-specific vocabulary as you can, as well as interesting expressions. For help with this, see my *Steps to a Higher Grade* document (**page 120**), and use it to come up with ideas of your own.

Mistakes are not the end of the world, and perfection is not expected at GCSE level, so be **bold** with your answers and try not to just give the bare minimum response. Instead, look to **extend** your sentences with conjunctions such as *weil, deshalb, auch, jedoch, zum Beispiel/beispielsweise* etc. You can also **link** various ideas with *einerseits/andererseits, im Vergleich/Gegensatz zu, obwohl* etc. in order to get your point across in an **interesting and convincing** way.

Finally, practice makes perfect! Practise with friends, teachers and others to gain confidence, as well as practising your German accent so that everything you say can be understood.

Interaction and Spontaneity

0	• No rewardable material.
1-3	• Candidate only occasionally responds spontaneously, and is often stilted, but with some examples of natural interaction. • Candidate occasionally initiates conversation and independently develops ideas, but requires frequent prompting. • Candidate occasionally sustains communication, with frequent hesitation.

4-6	• Candidate responds spontaneously to some questions, with natural interaction for parts of the conversation. • Candidate initiates and independently develops the conversation sometimes, with some prompting needed. • Candidate sometimes sustains communication, sometimes with rephrasing, self-correction or repairing phrases, and with some hesitation.
7-9	• Candidate responds spontaneously to most questions, with natural interaction for most parts of the conversation. • Candidate mostly initiates and independently develops the conversation. • Candidate sustains communication throughout most of the conversation, sometimes with rephrasing, self-correction or repairing phrases if needed, and with occasional hesitation.
10-12	• Candidate responds spontaneously and with ease to questions, resulting in natural interaction throughout. • Candidate consistently initiates and independently develops the conversation. • Candidate sustains communication throughout, rephrasing or using repair strategies if necessary to continue the flow, with minimal hesitation.

Again, it is clear from the mark scheme that your answers don't have to be perfect: the exam is intended to mimic a real-life conversation and has to sound **natural**. Therefore, a bit of hesitation and pausing is to be expected. Likewise, don't rush through your answers at break-neck speed, as this sounds unnatural. Do, however, respond **promptly** to the question.

You are also expected to **help** the conversation along, and develop it. So **add in your own ideas** and **lead the discussion** towards issues that you know how to talk about. In this way, you can guide your examiner to questions you have practised. Don't just give the bare minimum response!

If you do make a mistake, or need a bit more time to understand the question, you can use **repair phrases**, such as those below. Make sure to keep speaking in German though – **never** revert to English or another language! This way, you can still convey your answer, even when you are struggling. For example:

Können Sie bitte diese/die Frage wiederholen? = Please can you repeat the question?
Können Sie bitte die Frage noch einmal langsam/auf eine andere Weise sagen? = Can you say the question again more slowly/in another way?
Was haben Sie gesagt? = What did you say?
Was meinen Sie damit?/Was soll das heißen? = What do you mean by that?
Also, lass mich darüber nachdenken... = Well, let me think about that...
Was für eine schwierige/interessante Frage! = What a difficult/interesting question!

Ich habe nie darüber nachgedacht, aber... = I have never thought about that before, but…
(Lassen Sie mich erklären) Was ich meine… = (Let me explain) What I mean…
Ich habe das aus Versehen gesagt. = I said that by mistake.

Try not to rely on these phrases, but you can use them if you are struggling and need a bit of help or time to think.

Linguistic Knowledge and Accuracy

0	• No rewardable material.
1-3	• Candidate manipulates a limited variety of mainly straightforward grammatical structures, with minimal use of complex structures. • Candidate uses some accurate grammatical structures, and some successful past, present and future tense conjugations, although with some ambiguity. • Candidate sustains sequences of coherent speech, although errors often hinder clarity of communication and meaning.
4-6	• Candidate occasionally demonstrates a variety of grammatical structures, with some use of complex structures, although with frequent repetition. • Candidate uses generally accurate grammatical structures, and generally successful past, present and future tense conjugations. • Candidate sustains generally coherent speech, although with errors that sometimes hinder clarity of communication and meaning.
7-9	• Candidate manipulates a variety of grammatical structures, with some variety of complex structures. • Candidate uses predominantly accurate grammatical structures, and mostly successful past, present and future tense conjugations. • Candidate sustains predominantly coherent speech, with errors rarely hindering clarity of communication and meaning.
10-12	• Candidate manipulates a wide variety of grammatical structures, with frequent use of complex structures. • Candidate uses consistently accurate grammatical structures, and consistently successful past, present and future tense conjugations. • Candidate sustains fully coherent speech, with errors not hindering clarity of communication and meaning.

Therefore, try and use complex structures in your responses. Use the *Steps to a Higher Grade* document to help with this.

You are expected to attempt to use longer sentences, with a range of parts of speech, such as pronouns, conjunctions, adverbs and adjectives, and to **avoid repetition** where possible. Also, you must try and provide a range of tenses when prompted: if the question is about your future plans, you must answer with the future tense; if it is about your past experiences, you must answer in the past!

Even this section of the mark scheme, which focuses on accuracy of language, <u>does not require error-free German</u>! Nevertheless, any errors must not get in the way of your meaning. You can come back and self-correct if you like, or rephrase what you are trying to say. Occasionally incorrect gender or adjectival agreements aren't major, mark-losing errors. However, using the incorrect **person** or **tense** with a verb can often be confusing to the examiner and will be penalised. Also, make sure that you answer the question you are asked – talking about something unrelated will be construed as a mistake!

To Sum Up:

As with the writing questions (see **Volume 2: Reading, Writing, Translation**), some **golden rules** will help you achieve a top mark in the oral exam:

- ✓ Use **past, present, and future tenses**, including with irregular verbs.
- ✓ **Justify** your opinions.
- ✓ **Don't be boring**! Maintain the conversation and use interesting vocabulary and a wide variety of structures, with minimal repetition.

The Recordings

Now listen to the recordings of mock oral exams featuring a real GCSE student (see **www.rsleducational.co.uk/germanaudio**). They cover **three** conversation topics, though in your exam you will probably only have time for two – or perhaps even one, if your answers are detailed enough! The marks I have given each recording are quite severe, for the sake of highlighting the strengths and weaknesses of different approaches.

Recording A – Topic Area: Hobbies and Leisure

In this recording, the student gives short, albeit accurate answers. By expanding his answers and providing more information in answer to every question, he could score much higher marks for Content. There are some pronunciation errors and occasionally a little hesitation – which is fine at this level. His intonation and accent are generally quite accurate (although pronunciation won't be penalized unless it makes things hard to understand), and he uses some complex structures, such as *es wäre gut…* He also proves that he can manipulate past tenses and he justifies his opinions regularly. There are very few errors, but the vocabulary is fairly basic, particularly at the beginning of the recording. Bear in mind that starting strongly provides confidence both to yourself and the examiner. Be ready with linking phrases to make your sentences longer, use more complex phrases and structures, and incorporate higher-tier vocabulary. Also, be prepared to give (roughly speaking) three points of information for each question: over-preparing and saying too much is **always** better than under-preparing and not saying enough, even if this means more mistakes!

Communication/Content	7
Spontaneity/Interaction	10
Linguistic Knowledge/Accuracy	10
Total (Out of 36)	27

Recording B – Topic Area: School and Education

This is a shorter topic, with fewer questions asked. The student could expand on many of his answers, although he only does so on occasion. *If in doubt, expand!* This is preferable to an uncomfortable silence when the examiner is unsure whether you've finished or not, or has to prompt you for more information. Again, the language used here is generally accurate, because is it fairly simple – although he does prove that he can use the conditional tense and some subordinating clauses (*weil, wenn* etc.). To boost his mark, he could show initiative by expanding his answers throughout, use past and future tenses where appropriate, and add more complex linguistic structures, such as a *wenn* clause or a subjunctive phrase. He does well in often repeating the language of the question so that his answers address it directly. This method also gives him a little more time to think about each answer! His intonation is a little odd at times, and further practice would help him to sound more fluent. However, he makes himself understood, so doesn't lose marks for this.

Communication/Content	8
Spontaneity/Interaction	11
Linguistic Knowledge/Accuracy	10
Total (Out of 36)	29

Recording C – Topic Area: Home and Abroad

In this conversation, the student responds well to each question, often expanding on his answers and providing several, different pieces of information. For top marks, he could try giving **even more** information, possibly expanding into other themes. For example, after he has said what he likes about his area, he might mention what his favourite place is, where he used to live, his ideal home, or something of that sort. Initiative and ambition are usually rewarded! On one occasion, his answer isn't detailed enough (what activities he did on holiday last year) and he is asked to expand, while his first few answers – although often expanded – involve fairly basic language. Once he gets going, he does start to use some very good structures including *wenn ich … hätte* and idioms such as *andere Länder andere Sitten*. Nonetheless, showing this linguistic knowledge and mastery of complex structures throughout would have been even better!

Communication/Content	10
Spontaneity/Interaction	11
Linguistic Knowledge/Accuracy	10
Total (Out of 36)	31

Example questions

The following list is not exhaustive, but it demonstrates the range of questions likely to be asked by your teacher/examiner.

They are designed to test your **vocabulary** and your ability to **express and justify** your opinions, as well as your ability to employ the **present, past, and future tenses** when appropriate. Use them to practise!

Different exam boards have different topic headings, and questions may be phrased differently, but they all ultimately cover the same material. Prepare for everything!

Topic Area A – Home and Abroad

- ➢ Wo wohnst du? Wie findest du es?
- ➢ Wie ist das Wetter?
- ➢ Was kann man in deiner Stadt/Region machen und sehen?
- ➢ Wie hat sich deine Region in den letzten paar Jahren verbessert?
- ➢ Wo möchtest du vielleicht in der Zukunft wohnen?
- ➢ Wo verbringst du normalerweise deinen Urlaub?
- ➢ Beschreibe deinen letzten Urlaub.
- ➢ Was wirst du im nächsten Urlaub machen?
- ➢ Was ist dein ideales Reiseziel? Warum?
- ➢ Ist es wichtig, ins Ausland zu fahren?
- ➢ Wie wichtig ist der Tourismus für die Zukunft deiner Region?
- ➢ Warum kann der Tourismus manchmal negativ sein?
- ➢ Was sind die Vor- und Nachteile vom Leben in der Stadt/auf dem Land?
- ➢ Verbringst du deine Ferien lieber mit deinen Freunden oder deiner Familie? (Warum?)
- ➢ Was gibt es für interessante Traditionen/Feste in deinem Land?
- ➢ Sind solche Traditionen wichtig?

Topic Area B – Education and Employment

- Beschreibe deine Schule.
- Beschreibe deine Schulroutine.
- Wie könnte man den Schultag verbessern?
- Wie fährst du zur Schule?
- Welche Studienfächer magst du (nicht)? Warum (nicht)?
- Was trägst du in der Schule? Bist du für oder gegen eine Schuluniform? Warum?
- Was hältst du von den Regeln deiner Schule? Haben sie sich neulich geändert?
- Was magst du (nicht) an deiner Schule?
- Glaubst du, dass Hausaufgaben wichtig sind?
- Was hast du gestern in der Schule gemacht?
- Beschreibe eine Klassenfahrt, die du gemacht hast.
- Was sind deine Pläne für die Zukunft?
- Ist es wichtig, auf die Uni zu gehen?
- Was wäre dein idealer Job?
- Beschreibe dein Praktikum.
- Denkst du, dass das Praktikum (/Berufserfahrung) notwendig ist?
- Warum haben viele Jugendliche einen Wochenendjob?
- Deiner Meinung nach, wird es schwierig für dich sein, in der Zukunft Arbeit zu finden?

Topic Area C – House, Home and Daily Routine

- Beschreibe deine Familie.
- Beschreibe wo du wohnst.
- Beschreibe deine tägliche Morgenroutine.
- Kommst du mit deiner Familie gut aus?
- Was machst du normalerweise mit deinen Freunden?
- Was hast du letztes Wochenende gemacht?
- Was machst du, um deinen Eltern zu Hause zu helfen?
- Warum ist es wichtig, dass junge Menschen zu Hause helfen?
- Was isst du üblicherweise in der Woche?
- Esst du und deine Familie gesundes Essen?
- Beschreibe das letzte Mal, als du in einem Restaurant gegessen hast.
- Was ist wichtiger - Familie oder Freunde?

Topic Area D – The Modern World and the Environment

➤ Was machst du zu Hause/in der Schule, um der Umwelt zu helfen?

➤ Warum ist es wichtig, der Umwelt zu helfen? Was sind die Konsequenzen, wenn wir die Umwelt nicht schützen?

➤ Warum recyceln manche Leute nicht gern?

➤ Fährst du oft mit öffentlichen Verkehrsmitteln? Was sind die Vor- und Nachteile?

➤ Wie wichtig ist es für dich, ein gutes Verkehrsmittel in deiner Region zu haben?

➤ Benutzt du soziale Netzwerke?

➤ Wann benutzt du dein Handy/deinen Computer? (In der Schule/zu Hause?)

➤ Welche Rolle spielt das Fernsehen in deinem Leben? Was für Sendungen wirst du heute Abend sehen?

➤ Beschreibe dein(e) Lieblingsfernsehsendung/Film/Buch.

➤ Warum ist es wichtig, Nachrichten zu verfolgen? Ist es besser, sie im Internet zu verfolgen oder in der Zeitung zu lesen?

➤ Schaust du Filme lieber im Kino oder im Fernsehen?

➤ Was sind die Vor- und Nachteile der Technologie/des Internets?

➤ Wie wichtig ist das Internet in deinem Leben?

Topic Area E – Social Activities, Fitness and Health

➤ Was ist dein Lieblingstag im Jahr? Warum?

➤ Beschreibe deinen letzten Geburtstag.

➤ Warum ist es gut für dich, zusammen mit deiner Familie zu feiern?

➤ Was machst du in deiner Freizeit?

➤ Was machst du üblicherweise nachmittags/an den Wochenenden?

➤ Gehst du gerne einkaufen? Wie oft? Was kaufst du?

➤ Was machst du, um dich fit zu halten?

➤ Beschreibe ein ideales Wochenende. Was würdest du machen?

➤ Welche Hobbys und Interessen hast du?

➤ Magst du Sport? Warum ist es wichtig, jeden Tag ein bisschen Sport zu machen?

➤ Welchen Sport hast du gern als kleines Kind getrieben?

➤ Magst du Musik? Was für Musik hörst du gern?

➤ Gehst du oft einkaufen? Was hast du mit deinem Taschengeld gekauft?

➤ Ist es besser, über das Internet einzukaufen?

➤ Hast du einen gesunden Lebensstil?

➤ Wie wichtig sind Essen und Trinken in deinem Leben?

➤ Warum sind manche Leute Vegetarier?

➤ Was hältst du von Rauchen/Alkohol/Drogen?

Steps to a Higher Grade

How to boost your written and oral responses

This section contains tips for raising the quality of your written and oral work and achieving a better grade. Try and incorporate several into each piece of work. You don't have to use all of these ideas in an answer, but it's a good idea to sprinkle them liberally throughout.

Meanwhile, prepare a checklist of things that you often get wrong and quickly write it out at the top of the exam paper before you start. This way you will know what to look for when you check your answers.

If I were to condense this list to **five essential steps**, they would be:

1) Past tenses
2) Future tenses
3) Justified Opinions
4) Correct sentence structure
5) Don't be boring!

Revise all tenses, including the present! The examiners will assume that you can conjugate verbs in the present tense without too many difficulties, but there can be some tricky things to consider:

> Irregular verbs – study the verbs *sein, gehen, haben, nehmen, tun, werden, wissen.*
> Weak and strong verbs.
> Verbs with a vowel change in the present or past tense e.g. *fahren: ich fahre, du fährst, er fährt, wir fahren, ihr fahrt, sie fahren.*
> Verbs that have prepositions e.g. *glauben an, hoffen auf, warten auf.*
> Separable and inseparable verbs.
> Reflexive verbs.
> Verbs that take the dative case e.g. *danken, folgen, gefallen, helfen.*
> Modal verbs: *dürfen, können, mögen, müssen, sollen, wollen.*
> The imperative (for orders and instructions).

The written and oral assessments are judged according to:

- Communication and Content
- Knowledge and Application of Language
- Accuracy

Use the tenses and structures in the following list whenever you have the opportunity.

1. Past tenses and when to use them

a) The (Present) Perfect Tense

Use the past participle of the main verb and an auxiliary verb (*haben* or *sein*) in the present tense to express a (recently) <u>completed action in the past</u>.

TOP TIP: *Haben* **or** *sein*?

It is often very difficult for learners of German to understand which verbs take *haben* or *sein* in the Perfect Tense, but there are some rules that will help you:

- A verb of motion (going or arriving anywhere), it is very likely to use **sein**.
- A verb that indicates changing position or state, e.g. getting up or lying down, is likely to use **sein**.
- If a verb is transitive i.e. has a direct effect on something else (an object), then it is likely to use **haben**.

You then have to form the past participle of the main verb:

Forming the Past Participle

In German, this is usually done by adding *ge-* to the stem of the verb and then adding *-t* (or *-et*) for weak verbs and *-en* for strong verbs.

Some verbs also have a vowel change in the stem.

Verbs ending in *–ieren* change their ending to *-iert* but don't take a prefix.

Separable verbs add *ge-* between the prefix and the main verb.

Inseparable verbs (with the following prefixes: *be-, emp-, ent-, er-, ge-, ver-,* or *zer-*) do not add *ge-* but they do still add *-t* or *-en*. These two types of verbs can be strong or weak.
spielen —> gespielt
machen —> gemacht
fahren —> gefahren
singen —> gesungen
denken —> gedacht
studieren —> studiert
abfahren —> abgefahren
unterbringen —> untergebracht
besuchen —> besucht
gefallen —> gefallen

The past participle goes at the end of the clause, unless in a dependent clause where the main verb is sent to the end, such as in the final example given below. (See the **Correct Sentence Structure** section below for more details).

Hast du etwas gehört? = Did you hear something?
Ich bin nach Deutschland gereist. = I travelled to Germany.
Wir haben Hunger gehabt, als wir in London gewesen sind. = We were hungry when we were in London.

b) The Preterite/Imperfect Tense

This tense is less common in German than it is in English, apart from **in writing**. The perfect tense (above) is more widely used than this tense to express past events, especially in conversation, but this is still an important tense to know.

Use this tense in German to describe a completed action or series of actions in the past, especially in written narratives, OR with the verbs *haben (hatte, hatten), sein (war, waren)* and modal verbs (**see page 123**) in conversation.

Sie fragten den Lehrer, aber er wusste es nicht. = She asked the teacher but he didn't know.
Er öffnete die Tür und wir rannten ins Haus. = He opened the door and we ran into the house.
Ich machte keine Reise, als ich krank war. = I didn't go on a trip whilst I was ill.
Während ich die ganze Nacht schlief, trank sie Kaffee. = While I slept the whole night, she drank coffee.
Es gab nichts zu essen. = There was nothing to eat.
Jedes Wochenende spielten wir Fußball im Park. = We used to play football in the park every weekend.

c) The Pluperfect (Past Perfect) Tense

Use this tense to express a completed action <u>far in the past</u>, by using the imperfect tense of the auxiliary verb (*sein* or *haben* – see above) and the past participle of the main verb:

Ich hatte das Lied nie gehört. = I had never heard the song.
Er hatte nichts gegessen. = He hadn't eaten anything.
Meine Eltern waren zu Hause geblieben, nachdem ich nach Deutschland gefahren war. = My parents had stayed at home after I had gone to Germany.

2. Future tenses

There are a couple of ways to talk about things in the future in German. Try to use at least **three** examples when speaking/writing about future events.

a) The Future Tense

Use *werden* in the present tense followed by the infinitive to talk about something that WILL (or probably will) happen. Just like in the perfect and pluperfect tenses, the main verb is sent to the end of the clause, unless in a dependent clause.

*Ich **werde** dich nie **vergessen**.* = I will never forget you.
*Ich hoffe, dass du **mitkommen wirst**.* = I hope that you will come too.
*Du hast viel Arbeit zu tun und du **wirst** wohl sehr müde **sein**.* = You have a lot of work to do and you'll probably be very tired.

b) The Conditional Tense

Similar to the future tense (above), use the auxiliary verb (*werden*) in the subjunctive (*Konjunktiv II*), i.e. *würden*, followed by the infinitive, to talk about something that WOULD happen, or for polite requests.

*Ich **würde** dieses Auto nie **kaufen**!* = I would never buy this car!
***Würdest** du mir bitte **helfen**?* = Would you please help me?

c) Modal Verbs

When used with a modal verb, the main verb occurs at the end of the clause, except when in a dependent clause. Modal verbs can be used in any tense (in the list below, the present tense is used, except where stated otherwise). A modal verb doesn't in itself create a future tense, but modal verb constructions can be used to discuss future events ("I have to work tomorrow").

dürfen – to be allowed to (*ich darf, dürfte*)
können – to be able to (*ich kann, könnte*)
mögen – to like to (*ich mag, möchte*)
müssen – to have to (*ich muss, müsste*)
sollen – to ought to, be supposed to (*ich soll, sollte*)
wollen – to want to (*ich will, wollte*)

***Darf** man hier rauchen?* = Is one allowed to smoke here?
*Er **kann** gut Deutsch (sprechen).* = He can speak German well.
*Ich **mag** das nicht tun.* = I don't like doing that.

*Ich **muss** jetzt arbeiten.* = I have to work now.
*Wir **sollen** etwas mitbringen.* = We are supposed to bring something.
*Meine Freundin **will** ins Kino (gehen).* = My girlfriend wants to go to the cinema.
*Er **durfte** nicht kommen.* = He was not allowed to come. (Past)
*Wir **konnten** nichts verstehen.* = We couldn't understand anything. (Past)
*Ich werde daran denken **müssen**.* = I will have to think about it. (Future)
*Ich **möchte** das nicht tun.* = I would not like to do that. (Conditional)

3. Expressing Justified Opinions

It's not enough to simply say whether you like something: you have to say **why**, or why not)! Try to offer at least **three** justified opinions, expressed in a variety of ways.

a) Express your opinions

Use a variety of the following examples to introduce your point of view (remember to use correct word order after these phrases):

> *Ich denke/Ich glaube (nicht), dass…* = I (don't) think that...
> *Meiner Meinung nach…/Nach meinem Ermessen…/Meines Erachtens…/Ich bin der Meinung/Ansicht, dass…/* = In my opinion/According to me/I am of the opinion that…
> *Ich mag/liebe (nicht) …* = I (don't) like/love…
> *Ich halte NOUN für ADJECTIVE…* = I think … is …
>   e.g. *Ich halte meine Schwester für ärgerlich.* = I think my sister is annoying.
> *Es gefällt mir (nicht)* = I (don't) like it.

b) Justify them!

Don't forget to explain why you feel that way! Don't just use *weil* – find other ways of justifying your opinions, using interesting adjectives wherever possible.

> *Da* = Since
> *Denn* = Since/For… NB *denn* doesn't send the verb to the end, unlike *weil* and *da* – use "normal" word order – see **Point 4) Correct Sentence Structure**.
> *Wegen* + genitive = Because of

Ich mag Deutsch, weil es wirklich nützlich ist. = I like German because it is really useful.
Ich halte meine Schule für faszinierend, denn man kann viel lernen. = I find my school fascinating, for one can learn a lot.
Ich habe es wegen meiner Mutter getan. = I did it for/because of my mother.

4. Correct Sentence Structure

Before we look at useful phrases and grammatical twists to boost the quality of your German, here is a quick summary of correct **word order** in German with the **Six Golden Rules of Sentence Structure**:

a) Main Verb, Second Idea

The main verb of the sentence should be the second idea of the sentence (not necessarily the second word!); known for short as MV2.

Ich habe eine Schwester. = I have a sister.
 1   2   3

In meinem Haus gibt es einen Computer. = In my house there is a computer.
 1   2   3   4

In other words, if the sentence starts with anything other than the subject, then verb comes next, and then the subject.

Gestern habe ich nichts gemacht. = Yesterday I did nothing.
   1   2   3   4   (2)

In the above example, the past participle also goes to the end of the sentence (see **Past tenses**, page 121).

b) Subordination

Many conjunctions (*weil, dass, obwohl, wann, als* etc.) send the verb <u>to the end of the clause</u>.

*Ich spiele Tennis, **weil** es aktiv **ist**.* = I play tennis because it is active.

*Es ist wichtig, **dass** wir etwas für die Umwelt **machen**, **weil** es uns alle **angeht**.* = It is important that we do something for the environment because it affects us all. (See also **Separable Verbs** on page 126).

c) Verb, Comma, Verb

When a conjunction (such as *wenn*) sends a verb to the end of the clause and this clause is followed by a comma, <u>the next clause is inverted</u>, with the verb occurring immediately after the comma.

*Wenn das Wetter schön **ist, fahre** ich mit dem Auto.* = When the weather is nice, I travel by car.

d) Time, Manner, Place

Otherwise known as *Wann? Wie? Wo?*, this rule means that there is a correct order for phrases that involve time (*Wann?*), the manner in which the verb is/was done (*Wie?*), and place or destination (*Wo?*). Not every sentence will contain all three, but those that do follow this order: Time, Manner, Place.

Ich fahre <u>morgen</u> <u>mit dem Auto</u> nach <u>Paris</u>. = Tomorrow I am driving by car to Paris.
          Time   Manner   Place

Ich bin <u>letzte Woche</u> <u>in London</u> gewesen. = Last week I was in London.
         Time   Place

e) Separable Verbs

Separable verbs (*trennbare Verben*) are very common in German and are made up of a preposition and the infinitive of a (usually common) verb, which together create a new word.

In a main clause, the verb splits into two, with the prefix (the first part) going to the end of the clause:

<u>Zusammen</u>leben = to live together
=> *Er lebt mit seiner Freundin <u>zusammen</u>.* = He lives with his girlfriend.

<u>Aus</u>kommen = to get on with
=> *Sie kommt mit ihrem Onkel gut <u>aus</u>.* = She gets on well with her uncle.

When using the future tense, the conditional tense, or modal verbs, the infinitive of the verb goes to the end of the clause **in its entirety**.

*Sie **muss** nächste Woche <u>ausziehen</u>.* = She has to move out next week.

*Sie **wollen** in ihrer neuen Wohnung <u>zusammenleben</u>.* = They want to live together in their new flat.

*Ich **werde** am Wochenende <u>ausgehen</u>.* = I will go out next weekend. (Future)

*Ich **würde** morgen <u>aufstehen</u>, wenn ich einen guten Job hätte.* = I would get up next morning, if I had a good job. (Conditional)

f) Infinitive Constructions with Separable Verbs

With some conjunctions, you have to insert *zu* in between the two parts of the separable verb at the end of the clause:

- ### *Um … zu* = In order to…

Um *rechtzeitig* <u>*aufzustehen*</u>*, brauche ich einen Wecker.* = In order to get up on time, I need an alarm clock.

Um *mit seiner Freundin* <u>*zusammenzuleben*</u>*, muss er eine Wohnung kaufen.* = In order to live with his girlfriend, he has to buy a flat.

If adding a new clause, don't forget **Rule (c), Verb comma Verb!**

- ### *Versuchen, (zu)* = To try (to)

Ich ***versuche*** *immer, um 7 Uhr* <u>*aufzustehen*</u>*.* = I always try to get up at 7 o'clock.

- ### *Hoffen* = To hope

Sie ***hofft***, *nächstes Jahr nach Mexico* <u>*auszuwandern*</u>*.* = She hopes to emigrate to Mexico next year.

- ### <u>*Vorhaben*</u> = To intend to

Sie ***hat vor***, <u>*in Birmingham umzusteigen*</u>*.* = She intends to change (trains) in Birmingham.

Note that <u>*vorhaben*</u> is itself a separable verb!

See **TOP TIP: Forming the Past Participle** on Page 121 for conjugating separable verbs in the Perfect Tense.

Wir <u>***haben***</u> *das Fenster* <u>***aufgemacht***</u>*.* = We opened the window.
Ich <u>***habe***</u> *meine Mutti* <u>***angerufen***</u>*.* = I called my mother.
Er <u>***ist***</u> *gestern* <u>***zurückgefahren***</u>*.* = He returned yesterday.

5. Don't be boring!

Keep your answers as interesting as possible. Here are some tips:

a) Interesting adjectives

When you come across adjectives that you find interesting, write them down here! This is just a starting point: develop this resource in your other notes.

verblüffend = amazing		
lebensnotwendig = essential		

b) Interesting adverbs: *Sehr —> wirklich, wahrlich, extrem, äußerst* etc.

Similar to the above point, instead of a "boring" adverb like *sehr* (very), try more interesting intensifiers such as those above (really; truly; extremely; especially). When you come across more, write them down here so that you can refer to – and learn – them!

außergewöhnlich	
äußerst	
besonders	

c) Avoid repetition.

Think of synonyms and more interesting ways to express yourself without repetition.

Instead of this ...

Ich mag Fußball spielen, weil es Spaß macht. Ich mag auch Musik, vor allem Rockmusik, weil es mehr Spaß als klassische Musik macht.
(= I like to play football because it's fun. I also like music, especially rock music, because it's more fun than classical music.)

... why not try this:

Ich spiele gern Fußball und ich trainiere dreimal pro Woche, weil es so viel Spaß macht. Außerdem habe ich eine Leidenschaft für viele Arten von Musik, obwohl ich Rockmusik am liebsten höre, da ich sie für viel aufregender als klassische Musik halte.

(= I really like playing football and I train three times a week because it's so much fun. Also, I am passionate about many types of music, although my favourite genre is rock music as I find it a lot more exciting than classical music.)

Notice how the second version is immediately more interesting. This will impress the examiner, as well as making it easier to remember than something boring.

d) Reduce the number of simple verbs.

For example, instead of this…

Ich habe das Käsebrot gegessen, weil ich großen Hunger hatte.
= I ate the cheese sandwich, because I was very hungry.

… why not try:

Ich habe das Käsebrot aufgefressen, weil ich halb verhungert war.
= I gobbled up the cheese sandwich, because I was almost dying of hunger.

Read widely, and take note of any unusual and interesting verbs.

e) Connecting words

Make sentences longer and more interesting by connecting them:

während = while, whereas
Wenn, wann, als = when
Relative pronouns (*der, die, das* etc.) = who, which

Or you can **expand on** or **explain** your previous sentence:

das heißt/anders gesagt = that is to say/in other words
zum Beispiel/beispielsweise/etwa = for example
deshalb = therefore
und so weiter = and so on/etc.

f) Use a variety of structures and vocabulary.

Boost the quality of your written and spoken German and keep it interesting! Here are some examples of constructions that examiners typically look for.

Haben structures
Ich habe Hunger. = I am hungry.

Wir hatten Furcht. = We were afraid.

Um…zu (+ verb) = In order to
Ich fuhr in die Großstadt, um Geschenke zu kaufen. = I drove into the city (in order) to buy presents.

Eben wollen = To be about to
Ich wollte eben ausgehen. = I was about to go out.

Dabei sein = To be in the middle of
Sie war dabei, ihre Sachen auszupacken. = She was in the middle of unpacking her things.

Weiter (machen) = To carry on (doing)
Sie sang weiter = She carried on singing

Nachdem + Pluperfect = After
Nachdem wir gegessen hatten, hatten wir keinen Hunger mehr. = After we had eaten, we weren't hungry anymore.

Seit (+ present tense) = for a period of time
Ich lerne Deutsch seit drei Jahren. = I have been learning German for three years.

Bei + Noun (dative) = On (doing something)
Bei unserer Ankunft… = On our arrival…

Bevor = Before (Sends the verb to the end)
Bevor ich etwas dafür tun konnte. = Before I could do anything about it.

Ohne zu + Infinitive = Without
Ohne zu wissen = without knowing
Ohne zu sprechen = without speaking

Negatives
Niemand = Nobody, no one
Nie = Never

Exclamations
Das ist unglaublich! = That's unbelievable!
Dass ich nicht lache! = Don't make me laugh!

Adjectives before nouns (these require the correct endings!)
ein komisch<u>er</u> Mensch
mit der neu<u>en</u> Ärztin

Comparatives
Das ist eine <u>bessere</u> Idee. = That is a better idea.

Superlatives
Das <u>schlimmste</u> Unglück. = The worst accident/luck.

Personal Pronouns
Sie erklärte es <u>mir</u>. = She explained it <u>to me</u>.

Impersonal verbs
Es geht mir gut. = It's going well (I'm doing well).
Es gefällt mir. = I like it (/It pleases me).
Es wundert mich. = It surprises me.

Sich entschliessen/den Entschluss machen + zu = To decide/make the decision to
Wir haben uns (dazu) entschlossen, dahin zu gehen. = We decided to go in.
Wir machten den Entschluss, mit ihnen nicht zu sprechen. = We made the decision not to speak to them.

Quoting direct speech between speech marks (plus inversion of verb)
>>Es tut mir Leid<< sagte er. = "Sorry", he said.

Man = 'One'/'You'
Man weiß nie. = One never knows.

Modal verbs: *dürfen, können, mögen, müssen, wollen, sollen*
See Modal verbs on Page 123.

Du sollst die Wahrheit sagen. = You ought to tell the truth.
Ich muss heute zu Hause bleiben. = I have to stay at home today.

Trotz (+ Genitive) = In spite of/despite
Trotz mein<u>es</u> Erstaunen<u>s</u> = Despite my astonishment

Idioms and expressions
Morgen ist auch ein Tag! = Tomorrow is another day!

Andere Länder andere Sitten. = Different countries, different customs.

Question words

Warum? = Why?
Wer? = Who?
Was? = What?
Wo? = Where?
Wann? = When?
Wie? = How?
Wozu? = Why? (What for?)

BONUS Konjunktiv (Subjunctive)

Although this is not *expected* at GCSE-level, it is worth learning a range of subjunctive phrases and using at least **one** in your work, because it may well earn you extra marks.

You use the first type of subjunctive (*Konjunktiv I*):

- in reported speech
- when there is an element of doubt

*Sie sagten, dass das Drehbuch nicht fertig **sei**.* = They said that the script is not ready.
*Der Schriftsteller sagt, es **sei** gut.* = The writer says it's good.
*Es gibt Gerüchte, dass eine neue Schauspielerin diskutiert **werde**.* = There are rumours that a new actress is being discussed.

OR you can use the *Konjunktiv II* to express the **Conditional Tense** and contrary-to-fact "if" clauses, i.e. wishes and hypotheses.

*Es **wäre** besser, wenn…* = It would be better if…
*Wenn ich nur das nicht **gemacht hätte**…* = If only I hadn't done that…
***Wärest** du früher **aufgestanden, hättest** du deinen Termin nicht **verpasst**.* = If you had woken up earlier, you wouldn't have missed the appointment.

6. Dos and Don'ts

Do

- ✓ Prepare a sentence for good AND bad weather in both the present and past tense.
- ✓ Prepare sentences for what you ate, did, played etc. in the past tense.
- ✓ Prepare positive concluding sentences, e.g. *Es hat viel Spaß gemacht.*
- ✓ … And negative concluding sentences, e.g. *Das hat mir nicht gefallen.*
- ✓ Plan each essay.
- ✓ Keep to the word limit.
- ✓ Leave five minutes after writing to check for mistakes.
- ✓ Write in the correct tense.
- ✓ Be consistent with your use of *du* (informal), *Sie* (polite) or *ihr* (informal, plural).
- ✓ Answer the question fully.
- ✓ Revise vocab, vocab, and more vocab!

Don't

- ✗ Over-complicate your ideas.
- ✗ Miss out accents.
- ✗ Forget punctuation and capital letters for nouns.
- ✗ Use Google translate or equivalent websites: they are not accurate enough.

BV - #0002 - 191119 - C6 - 297/210/7 - PB - 9781916193147